DISASTER READY PEOPLE FOR A DISASTER READY AMERICA

D0816170

By James W. Satterfield
& Harry W. Rhulen

Illustrations by Amy Rumbarger

We wrote this book, in part, as a response to the devastating effects of Hurricane Katrina, the 9/11 terrorist attacks, the 2005 tsunami and other similar events. After extensive study of the response to and aftermath of these crises, we realized that through proper planning much of the devastation experienced on both the human and corporate levels could have been mitigated or eliminated entirely. This book is designed to help individuals and families create a home disaster plan. We've evaluated the numerous exposures and situations of various disaster scenarios, including the looming pandemic threat, and developed this guide to assist you. If it starts you thinking, if it prompts you to take some action, we will have accomplished a lot. Work hard and prepare. Good luck. Remember: you are your own first responder.

Harry & Jim

TABLE OF CONTENTS

How to Get the Most Out of This Book   7

Introduction—What, Me Worry?   9

    Reasons to Not Prepare   9
    The Year Ahead   13
    Disaster Disparity: A Real Crisis   14

Disaster Preaction™—A Month by Month Plan   17

Chapter 1. Getting Started: The Conversation   17

    Kitchen Fire   17
    Water Main Break   18
    Disasters of a Regional or National Level   19
    Your Attitude Matters   20
    The Conversation   20
    Communications / Rendezvous   23
    Take inventory   24
    You and Your Utilities   25
    Your Preaction™ Plan—Put It In Writing   26
    Family Agreements   27
    Month 1 Action Plan   29

Chapter 2. Identify Your Risks   31

    Real Risks   32
    Identifying Zones   35
    Nuclear Power Plants   38
    Month 2 Action Plan   40

Chapter 3. Your Contact Lists   43

    Extended Family and Friends   43
    Emergency Services   44
    Business   45
    Month 3 Action Plan   45

Chapter 4. Your Family Communication Plan   49

    Who?… The Lead   49
    Where?… The Meeting Places   49
    Phone Tree Agreement   54
    Month 4 Action Plan   55

Chapter 5. Should You Stay…   57

    Water   57
    Food   61
    First Aid Kit   64
    Month 5 Action Plan   66

Chapter 6. Should You Go…   69

    Your Evacuation Kit   69
    Pack and Test   72
    Extra Evacuation Kits   72
    Month 6 Action Plan   74

Chapter 7. Your Evacuation Plan   75

    Evacuation Scenarios   76
    Disaster Planning at Work   77
    Evacuation from Work   77
    Evacuation from School   78
    Month 7 Action Plan   79

Chapter 8. Protecting Your Identity and Financial Interests   85

    Sources of Identity Theft   85
    If You're Victimized   89
    Month 8 Action Plan   91

Chapter 9. Medical Forms | 93

    Month 9 Action Plan | 94

Chapter 10. When You Travel | 97

    Before You Go... Think | 98
    Document and Distribute | 98
    Hotel Security | 99
    Packing | 102
    Alert and Confident | 102
    Month 10 Action Plan | 103

Chapter 11. Pandemics | 105

    What You Can Do | 108
    Month 11 Action Plan | 108

Chapter 12. Keeping Your Plan Current | 109

    Conversation and Practice | 109
    Practicing Your Plan | 109
    Month 12 Action Plan | 111

What's Next? | 113

After A Disaster | 113

Congratulations | 116

Disaster Preparedness—Resources | 117

Index | 120

Footnotes | 122

HOW TO GET THE MOST OUT OF THIS BOOK

This book has one goal: to help you and your family prepare for disaster. Like most people, you are probably in disaster denial. That is, although you are aware that a catastrophe of one sort or another is highly possible, you ignore its potential reality and figure you'll deal with it when the time comes. That time is now.

As you prepare for those disasters most likely to affect you, you will learn to do so as they uniquely pertain to you, based on specific risks to your location and lifestyle, and you will understand how you can prepare for and lessen their impact on you when they do occur. We will help you go from disaster denial to disaster Preaction™—the efforts you need to make (or motions you need to go through) before you are in the midst of a crisis. So, grab a pen and highlighter. You'll want to write in the margins, jot down reminders, and make other notes. In other words, own it! You are your own first responder.

Although you could read this book cover to cover, that may not be the best way. To get the most out of it, start with Part I, What, Me Worry? Then, review the Table of Contents for an overview of the preparations we recommend. Part II is divided into twelve chapters, ideally one for each month, so that by the end of one year, you will be disaster-ready. In the course of a dozen, easily paced steps, you will not become overwhelmed or discouraged. Each month builds upon the previous month's information, so you will cumulatively gain a solid foundation of how, why, where, and when to do what. (The "who" is you.)

Next, set aside a time to read and act on the advice in Part II, beginning with Chapter 1, Getting Started: The Conversation. This is your first call-to-action and will set the stage for the other eleven chapters and action-items. A quick approach to staying on track and ensuring you follow through with all twelve steps is to make a contract with yourself... schedule a non-negotiable time for you to come back to this book each month. Be honest and keep this commitment, as you would any other appointment.

From time to time in this process, we will direct you to web sites and other organizations for additional information. We included these web sites so your research time will be reduced.

What Is a Preaction™ Plan?

When you react, you behave thoughtlessly, irrationally, often making things worse. When you preact, you take time to think clearly and process possibilities, options and contingencies. You have a plan that enables you to perform well in an emergency.

Regardless of what is said or not in this book, you control your own disaster preparedness. No one is more interested in protecting you and your family than you are. And only you and your family truly understand your particular situation. To benefit from this book, evaluate its guidance based on your individual circumstances/position. Incorporate the best tactics and strategies that apply to you into a custom-made plan. As you tailor the suggestions to your own requirements, you gain the upper hand.

Despite best intentions, we may have left out some things. Do not hesitate to add anything that applies to you and your family that will favorably impact your preparation. Disregard whatever doesn't fit your situation. If you work through this book and do the steps as they are outlined here, by the end of the year, you'll have in place a personalized Preaction™ Plan. And, you will be armed with the confidence and skills necessary to calmly take on most any disaster.

Also note that the forms at the end of each chapter in the book can be downloaded from http://www.firestorm.com/book/forms.html. You might find it more convenient to fill them out on your computer and add the printed form to your plan.

INTRODUCTION—WHAT, ME WORRY?

★

WHAT, ME WORRY?

There is no dependence that can be sure
but a dependence upon one's self.
—John Gay

More than 2 million families experience some sort of disaster or major emergency every year. These incidences range from major events that simultaneously affect thousands of people, like the terrorist attacks of September 11, 2001, or the gulf coast's Hurricane Katrina in 2005, to individual catastrophes, like a serious traffic accident or a home fire. Yet less than half the families in America have taken a single step to prepare themselves for such misfortunes.

This lack of preparedness reflects a cavalier attitude and flat out denial of both unforeseen and predictable disturbances… what we refer to as the "What, me worry?" syndrome. On the other hand, this failure to prepare, against all types of warnings, is a sign of optimism.

In reality, we all know disasters can and do hit. And, one could strike you. Their probabilities and proven track records generate an underlying constant. This awareness is like a constant, low-level hum in the background of our lives. It's a source of worry and stress. Why do we not act? How is it that we don't prepare for emergencies? Those who ignore the need to prepare for emergencies give several reasons, including:

- *"I don't know what to do."*

- *"It will take too much time."*

- *"I can't afford it."*

- *"What's the point?"*

While there is a bit of truth in each thought, for the most part they simply aren't true on the whole. Let's take a quick look at each of these thoughts, in reverse order. Each objection has an equally powerful counter-argument that proves it can be done, that you can prepare!

"What's the Point?"

While we all admit we should be prepared for a disaster, to some degree at least, we also acknowledge there is no way to be ready for every eventuality. This discouraging thought tends to get generalized into thinking there's no point in doing any preparation at all. Switch gears now. In a more positive light, we can, in very basic strides, prepare for many emergencies. Here's how:

- *Water. Supply can be cut off without warning. So, fill several plastic gallon containers with water and store them under the sink. While you're at it, put additional containers in the trunk of each car.*

Time to prepare—low; Cost to prepare—low; Potential benefit—high.

- *Food. Granted, this will do you no good if your home is destroyed, but it will help in most other disasters.*

Time to prepare—low; Cost to prepare—low; Potential benefit—high.

- *Evacuation Plan. Often you don't know what kind of disaster to expect, so you can't predict if you'll stay put or evacuate. Having a plan will facilitate a logical decision made calmly.*

Time to prepare—low; Cost to prepare—low; Potential benefit—high.

In summary, you really can do a great many things that will make a significant and positive difference for you and your family when a disaster is upon you. As with many of the suggestions, they involve minimal effort, time and money. It's a matter of changing your attitude and outlook… from one of chance to control.

"It Is Too Expensive."

Think large. Act small. When shifting our focus to preparing for a disaster, we unnecessarily pressure ourselves right away. This all-or-nothing thinking backfires: we end up doing nothing! However, if you approach preparation more constructively, in manageable pieces, regardless of budget, any of you can afford to prepare. Don't feel ineffective if you do not have enough money to buy a generator right now or have a place for one. Feel empowered that you can have on hand a couple of flashlights (and fresh batteries) and some long-burning candles. Other easily affordable items:

- *Plastic soda, water and similar containers for water storage. Rinse out those you acquire in your normal shopping, fill them with tap water and stash them away.*

- *Extra rations of peanut butter, protein bars, canned vegetables or dry cereal. These non-perishables can be a part of your emergency kit a long while before they must be replaced. Remember to have the can opener handy!*

- *Make sure everyone knows how and when to call 911.*

Sure, you can spend a lot of money preparing for a disaster, but it is not necessary. Many of the basic preparations of the most critical supplies can be at the ready very economically, often for or as little as $30.00 to $50.00.

"It Takes Too Much Time"

Another misconception. But, don't get wrapped up in the big picture. Rather, break down the problem into reasonable chunks of time and energy. No, you won't get completely prepared today or next week. Focus instead on what is at hand, on what you can make happen... on those individual motions that are part of the larger process. Soon enough, you will be there.

- *Decide where you're going to keep your emergency flashlights and candles. It can be in any cool, dark place, just so you and your family know where to look when the lights go out and/or the heat goes off.*

Time required: seconds

- *Add candles, waterproof matches a flashlight or two and extra batteries to your next shopping trip.*

Time required: less than 5 minutes

- *Schedule a time with your family to have a conversation about preparing for an emergency. An hour or so over dinner can mean the difference between chaos and calm during a disaster.*

Time required: 60–90 minutes

"I Don't Know What To Do"

While you undoubtedly don't know everything about preparing for a disaster, give yourself some credit! Even without this book, you do possess some basic knowledge:

- *Food and water are critical. Check. Now, step it up: learn how much you actually need and the details of long-term storage of each.*

- *Roads become parking lots in large-scale emergencies. So, step it up: learn to protect yourself and ride the disaster out at home (outside of mandatory evacuations).*

- *At times, evacuation is mandatory. No problem, step it up: learn the basics of an orderly exodus to safety.*

Preparing for disaster doesn't require a lot of study or survival expertise; nor is it esoteric. It is hands-on and pre-active. In fact, most disaster preparedness is common sense.

Preparing for Disaster Reduces Anxiety

Like it or not, disasters are a part of living, a natural order. Hardly a day goes by that you don't hear about some sort of calamity... earthquakes, fires, floods, storms, terrorism, etc. The media invites and encourages worry and stress. In fact, you are so bombarded with "fear messaging," you just shut it out as it could apply to you. You consciously avoid thinking about any potential harm to you, despite the nonstop stream of doom. But the uneasiness is there... you feel it, children feel it—everyone does. Yet, we can reverse course and turn that energy and misguided helplessness into preparation!

Starting this very moment, replace your preoccupation with preparation. Imagine how you would feel if you were fully prepared for a disaster right now. Your plans are in place, they've been updated during the last six months, and the critical supplies are within easy reach. You know what to do. Feeling confident, right? That is your goal.

It's Up To You

There's simply no way around it. Preparing for a disaster is your responsibility. Although the U.S. Department of Homeland Security, your state government, and your local government all plan to help in a disaster, the truth is you can't count on them being where you need them when you need them. The same thing is true for the power company, your land phone line company, your cell phone company, your internet provider and the water company; it's also even true for private agencies like the Red Cross. Each organization works hard to solve problems when disaster strikes, but that doesn't mean they'll be able to address your particular problems in a timely fashion.

You are your own first responder... Take charge now!

The sooner you start, the better, and you can start right now. We've made it easy for you.

The Year Ahead

What may not seem obvious about the range and depth of possible disasters is that you prepare for them in roughly the same way. The differences to consider are often regional or geographic in scope. For example, the West Coast of the United States is more likely to experience a major earthquake, while people living in Kansas are susceptible to yearly tornado seasons. Regardless of the location or disaster, you'll need:

- *Food and water.*

- *Family whereabouts and contact information.*

- *Candles, flashlights, batteries, matches and a battery-operated radio*

- *A decision and strategy on where to weather out the disaster.*

12-Step Outline

Our technique for getting prepared for a disaster involves 12 easy steps. Using the strategies set forth below, you can be ready in 12 months through a monthly series of preparations, each building upon the other. Each chapter that follows details one step.

1. Getting Started: The conversation

2. Identify Your Risks

3. Your Contacts List

4. Your Family Communication Plan

5. Should You Stay...

6. Should You Go...

7. Your Evacuation Plan

8. Identity and Financial Interest Protection

9. Medical forms

10. When You Travel

11. Epidemics to Pandemics

12. Keeping Your Plan Current

Okay, we've been a bit tricky. The 12th Step, in the 12th month of preparations, is the beginning of a life-long practice. On that day of every month, schedule a little time to review and update your personal Preaction™ Plan. Of course, you may choose any day of the month. Just make sure that whatever day you select, it's consistent (we suggest days 1–28), and that you stick with it.

Of course, you can accelerate your preparation, completing the steps in 12 days or 12 weeks. If you do, however, decide to speed up the process, be careful to not take on too much at once. Otherwise, you may stop, give up and never return! Just understand that a monthly routine of one chapter will get you in great shape for the next crisis.

Disaster Disparity: A Real Crisis

If you are poor, you are left out of most disaster plans. Surprised? In recent history, we have seen time and again that whatever disaster preparedness the country has managed to achieve, whether on local, state, regional or Federal levels, no plan seems to include the economically disadvantaged in any meaningful way. If you are part of this cross-section, many of the typical disaster preparations, particularly the evacuation plans, won't help you.

From another angle, if you don't have a car, you've got problems no matter what your income. It's understandable that, in a car-crazed nation that lacks adequate public transportation in all but perhaps three major metropolitan areas in the entire nation, cars would be a major part of every evacuation plan. Nevertheless, if you do not have access to a private vehicle, do not despair.

There are many things you can do in advance of a disaster to prepare in the event of one. This book, in an effort to address some of those identified shortcomings, seeks to educate you with simple, cost-effective suggestions, techniques and practices that will work for you and your family in a time of need.

It's tempting to label the des-equilibrium in preparedness (or preparedness inequality) a problem of racism, yet a broader perspective more accurately reveals the root of the problem as poverty, regardless of race, ethnicity or other categorization. For some living in the United States, poverty is only a paycheck away, especially in light of the cutthroat corporate downsizing and outsourcing… all to satisfy short-term shareholder value and Wall Street's whims, amidst an increasingly competitive global economy. Disasters tend to bring these economic gaps to the forefront, as they have an unfairly disproportional impact on those who can least afford a crisis.

Our intent with this book is to make disaster preparedness accessible to all, regardless of income, race, gender, disability or any other grouping. This book will be distributed widely among the disadvantaged to ensure such preparedness. This is a start, it is your start, to taking charge and being in control, to relying on yourself for you and your family's safety.

Disasters happen. Be your own first responder. We know you can and this book will show you how!

Jim & Harry

Jim Satterfield and Harry Rhulen

P.S. We look forward to hearing how you are doing and what you are doing as you prepare. Please let us know what has been the most helpful or insightful to you and feel free to forward us suggestions to improve on this book. You may write us at prepared@firestorm.com

DISASTER PREACTION™: A MONTH BY MONTH PLAN

★

1. GETTING STARTED

If it is to be, it is up to me
—William H. Johnsen

It can't be said too often, the responsibility for preparing for disaster is yours alone. This becomes clear if you think about what actually happens in a disaster. Let's look at a couple of strictly local situations:

Kitchen Fire

What happens if a fire breaks out in your kitchen? If it's a grease fire, water will only make it spread. You call 911 and help is on the way. Depending on where you live, help may take from 10 minutes to over an hour to arrive. A fire can do an amazing amount of damage in 10 minutes.

The statistics about fire are amazing. According to FEMA (Federal Emergency Management Agency) 2004:

- *3,900 civilians that lost their lives as the result of fire.*

- *17,785 civilians injured as the result of fire.*

- *117 firefighters killed while on duty.*

- *Fire killed more Americans than all natural disasters combined.*

- *83% of all civilian fire deaths occurred in residences.*

- *Fewer than 1.6 million fires were reported. Many others went unreported, causing additional injuries and property loss.*

- *Direct property loss due to fires was estimated at $9.8 billion with an estimated $714 million in property damage attributed to intentionally set structure fires.*

- *An estimated 36,500 intentionally set structure fires resulted in 320 civilian deaths.*

However, you're in control if you have a fire extinguisher and know how to use it. You'll be able to put out the fire before the fire trucks arrive. Without the extinguisher, you're best bet is to leave the house and await the fire department's arrival. What's preventing you from getting a fire extinguisher today for kitchen fires?

Water Main Break

Suppose, for a moment, that a major water line in your community breaks. Almost immediately, smaller water lines leading off the main lose water pressure; so does every home and business along those water lines. In fact, before long water delivery will quickly stop altogether in those areas.

The water company will probably notice the drop in pressure right away, but if the broken main is deep in the ground, they may have no idea where the break has actually occurred. Chances are, however, water will begin to surface soon near the site of the leak. The water company's first act will be to turn off water upstream from the break, which means even more homes and businesses will be without water.

Meanwhile, you've discovered you're getting air from your water pipes.

It will take an hour or so at least, and maybe a long as half a day or even longer for the water company to figure out exactly what they have to do to fix the break. You may not get accurate news of when to expect water for several hours, or even a full day.

As this situation develops, people begin rushing to stores to buy bottled water. It won't take too long before the supermarkets and convenience stores have sold all the water they have in stock. If it takes the water company more than a day or so to get the water flowing again, your city or town may be able to organize some water deliveries from outside the area. That will take additional time, and if they're successful, the additional water will dribble in at first and the cost of the water will increase.

You're in control, however, if you've got enough water stored for you and your family to get along for several days. You'll be able to cook, drink, bathe, and even do some light cleaning.

These two real examples are examples that happen every day in this country. Fires start in kitchens and water lines break. There are predictable delays before help arrives. If you are prepared with the right kind of fire extinguisher and stored water, both recoverable situations become minor nuisances. With a little preparation, you've moved from the position of a victim looking to other people for help, to being your own first responder.

Regional and National Level Disasters

Now, think about what happens when there's a big disaster like a major earthquake, a category 4 or 5 hurricane, a cluster of tornados, a wild fire that burns a thousand homes, a severe winter storm, an extreme heat wave in a large city, or a terrorist attack. It takes time for help to arrive, if indeed it ever comes. The process for the federal government to declare a disaster and begin to move help into an area is time-consuming. As it stands now, these are the steps:

1. First, the proper authority at the local level (mayor, town council, county board, etc.) must declare a disaster within 10 days of the event. In order for the disaster to be escalated to the state level, the Director of the Office of Emergency Services must concur. State and/or federal assistance will be provided only when the effects of the emergency are beyond the capability of local resources to effectively mitigate. During this process, prior to the declaration of a disaster, only local help is available, and unfortunately, the quality and quantity of local help varies tremendously.

2. The next step is for the Governor of the State(s) to declare a disaster. This lets the state(s) mobilize its (their) resources. Some Federal aid may be available at this point, but again, the caliber and availability of help varies widely from state to state.

3. If the disaster is large enough to warrant Federal assistance, the President of the United States must declare the situation a disaster; the President has between five and 30 days to make such a declaration, depending on the circumstances. How much help will be extended depends on the type of disaster, as well as the available (two incidences in one sentence!) resources.

Although most local authorities try to put together a plan for disaster, most local governments or agencies are sadly, inadequately equipped and poorly organized. Even if local disaster authorities are well organized, they, themselves, may be impacted by the disaster, thus reducing or eliminating their assistance altogether. Even when a community has a good plan, there's no way to be sure how well it will actually be implemented until a disaster strikes.

Your Attitude Matters

Your attitude towards disaster preparedness will determine the degree to which you successfully navigate an emergency. The first thing anyone feels in a disaster is fear and confusion... the "Why me?". If the disaster is sudden, you may feel panic. If the disaster is an event like an approaching hurricane, or wild fire, or even a gradually building extreme heat event or well predicted winter storm, anxiety and fear will build over time. The growing worry of a pandemic, as a result of what we're now calling bird flu or avian flu, is an example of a disaster that's extremely slow in developing. In the slow moving disasters, real fear or panic doesn't hit until it becomes obvious you're likely to be involved, but the anxiety is there.

It's your attitude, your state of mind, and your feelings that will determine how well you fare in a disaster or crisis.

When disaster strikes, if you've done nothing, your fear reaction will be higher than it needs to be; your thinking will be anything but clear and you'll act out of that fear. You're decisions are apt to be poor, even life-threatening.

On the other hand, when disaster strikes, if you have taken the time to think through how you will handle an emergency or a disaster, and taken the steps to be prepared, you'll feel far less fear and be able to think clearly and execute on decisions that you had planned for. The actions you take as a result of being prepared are likely to make your life much easier during the catastrophe, and quite possibly can save your life, as well as those of the ones you love.

The Conversation

The first thing you need to do to prepare for a disaster is to speak with your family and/or those with whom you live. If you live alone, have this conversation with yourself. But know you don't have to prepare all by yourself. Your family, friends, co-workers, colleagues, classmates, etc. will work with you; in fact, you're probably part of their extended team, too.

This conversation will address the low-level anxiety we all have about disaster and begin to change that anxiety into positive action.

The goal of the conversation is three-fold: to predict, to plan, and to perform.

Predict: To predict means to assess the risks you face. It's in the discovery of the risks that you could face that you'll begin to develop the solutions... your preparations. In the initial conversation, you won't know all the risks, but you'll know some of them and that's where you start.

Plan: Again, at this stage, your planning will probably be minimal. It's here you plan to plan. You get the dialogue going. Everyone is inspired and on-task, enthusiastic and increasingly confident of their ability to make a difference in their lives.

Perform: Do what it takes to make your plan real—that is, take the steps to get your plan in shape. Suggested topics in this first conversation include:

- *Acknowledge that a disaster can happen to you*

- *Discuss your personal vulnerabilities, including special risks your community faces (We'll talk more about this in a bit.) as well as any special needs your household has, such as pets, seniors, people with disabilities and/or babies or small children. (predict stuff)*

- *Setting some preliminary goals for continuing your disaster plans and preparations. (plan stuff)*

Figure you'll spend about an hour and a half with all the members of your household who are able to contribute. Gather together the adult members of your household first. Then, have a second conversation with the younger members, incorporating thoughts and ideas given at each level of comprehension. One way to start the conversation is to ask: "How would you feel if a disaster hit our home today?" or "What would you do if a disaster hit right this moment?" Let everyone say whatever comes up. You may be surprised to find out that your teenage son or daughter has some good ideas. Get the thoughts, concerns and fears out on the table. As the conversation moves along, the dialogue will open up, and you and others will feel more comfortable exposing your uncertainties and worries. In these first 90 minutes, do not make light of any of the fears or dismiss them; at this stage, any concerns are valid. You want an open and honest discussion. This effort now to foster cooperation and teamwork will naturally surface to work in your favor in a time of need.

The Disaster Preaction™ Teams:

Families With Infants And Young Children

If you have young children with little to no grasp of language, you obviously won't involve them in your conversations about disasters. But as soon as they are old enough to walk and talk, they should be involved in at least some of both the conversation and the preparations.

By then they are processing what they see and hear on television, read in newspaper and magazine captions and headlines, so they will be asking questions! In addition, they are likely to hear other kids or teachers talking about war or terrorism or the flu. Their pre-school may have a disaster plan (and communication of that in an age-appropriate context) and may on occasion conduct emergency drills. If you've not yet heard what your children's school or daycare has in place regarding a plan, inquire and get a copy. You might also review it with your child at home, since this would show consistency and instill confidence in your children that you will be calm under duress. They, in turn, will sense this control and will feel more comfortable and secure.

Families With Older Children

By the time your children are in first grade, they are participating in fire drills at school. At this stage, their school(s) may have a disaster plan, too; —ask about one. Don't underestimate what they know and their ability to contribute; including them is a must.

Once your children reach middle school and high school, they can participate more fully, as they have sense of what can go wrong in their world. As a teenager, they have some skills to evaluate an emergency or crisis and how best to respond to it.

Single Parents

If you are a single parent, you may at first think that talking about disaster preparedness is daunting. But, you are not alone. Teaming up with another single parent or two in your neighborhood to work on this will be mutually beneficial. Anyone else who is involved in the care of your children (babysitters, daycare workers, nannies, grandparents, etc.) should also be part of your conversations and plans.

Seniors

Depending on their age and their health, seniors may not be able to move as quickly or think as clearly as before, or they may become easily disoriented. However, experience is on their side, and they can contribute plenty to planning your response to a disaster. Make sure you take any limitations into consideration in preparing your plan.

Disabled Individuals

People with disabilities are no different than the extremely young or old in needing to be included in your conversations and planning. Individually assess each situation and their unique challenges accordingly, but don't underestimate their ability to understand, respond and contribute appropriately in a crisis.

Begin To Assess The Actual Risks You Face

This will lead naturally into a discussion of the risks you and your household actually face. You already know the outlines of the risks. You know, for example, if your community is at risk for hurricanes or tornados or earthquakes or wildfires. You probably know if you live in a flood zone (although this can be less obvious than you might think). You know, for example, that when a pandemic or global epidemic actually takes hold, everyone is at risk. You know that large cities and military installations are more likely to be targets of terrorism than rural areas. Begin by making a general list of the risks you know you're subject to. Include things like house fires, and traffic accidents.

Those are the obvious risks. You will need to do some research to discover other kinds of risks in your area. We will address how to find out about those risks in the next chapter.

Communications / Rendezvous

Wind up your first conversation with some concrete steps each of you can take the next day and the next week. Make a list of every family member and where s/he is in a typical week. Work schedules, school routines, camps, daycare, evening extracurricular classes, and carpool routes should be included. Of course, there will be exceptions for everyone (special school activities, vacations, business trips, etc.). Don't try to get every detail; the purpose is to capture the general whereabouts and patterns of each. In the event you need to find each other, should cell phone communication be out, you could meet up more quickly.

Often, this kind of information is already written elsewhere, on a calendar on the refrigerator or whiteboard. For your disaster plan purposes, transfer this information onto a smaller, portable format, such as an index card... one for each person. Or, write it in your agenda. For example:

- *Mom—works at (address of her work; telephone number, cell number, and email there) Mon—Fri. from 9 a.m. to 5. Commutes about 15 minutes each day along East First Street and often stops on the way home at the shopping center. Weekends she and dad run errands, often together.*

- *Dad—works at (address of his work; telephone number, cell number, and email there) Mon—Fri from 6:30 a.m. to 3:30. Commutes about 30 minutes each way, mostly on Interstate 8. On Tuesdays, stops at the gym (address and phone) for an hour.*

Write down their Social Security number and date and place of birth, too; these are required if you ever need to apply for disaster relief. You may also want to list your out-of-town relatives in the same manner. If your city or region is struck by a disaster, real time communications may be patchy at best. Your extended family members can be a critical part of your disaster response network. As they will probably not have been affected, ask them to use their cell or landline on your behalf.

Take Inventory

Determine what you have on hand now in the way of emergency supplies. Don't worry that the minute you prepare your next meal, the tally will be different. The point here is to record what you have and what you still need.

- *Flashlights, battery-operated radio, batteries, candles and matches or a lighter. Note what you have and where you keep them.*

- *Shelf-stable food. Canned, dry foods and other non-perishables last the longest. MRE's (Meals Ready-to-Eat that the military uses) are now available online, too, and they last for years. Food in your freezer will last up to 72 hours once the power is turned off, if you minimize the number of times the freezer door is opened. (Read more about food supplies in chapter 4)*

- *Cooktops. Barbecue grill, camp stove, butane tank or other potable fuel. Think about what you will need to make a warm meal.*

- *Medication. Jot down what you have on hand.*

You and Your Utilities.

In an emergency, you, yourself, might need to turn off your water, electricity, gas and security system. Make sure everyone old enough to shut off access knows how to do so:

- *Water main—should pipes in your home develop a leak. If you live in a house, the water main is usually at the street. If you live in a condominium or apartment, ask the manager how to turn off water to your unit.*

- *Electricity—electrical sparks and gas do not mix; they could cause explosions in proximity. The main electrical switch is usually in a metal-encased, breaker box, which may be in a garage, a closet or against an outside wall. It's often near the electrical meter.*

- *Gas—where the supply directly comes into your property.*

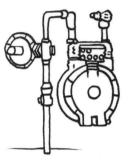

- *Home Security Systems—learn how to manually disengage your alarm system before you've got a ear canal busting ring that you cannot turn off, especially if the security company cannot locate anyone who knows the codes to determine that it has falsely gone off, whatever the trigger.*

Your Preaction™ Notebook

To get your written Preaction™ Plan working for you, create a Preaction™ Notebook. We recommend a 2-inch, 3-ring binder (you may have one you can reuse). You'll also need some dividers that allow you to slip in the name of each section in a tab. Much like you mark your luggage, make the cover distinctive so you can find it right away, and make sure everyone knows what it looks like. Decide now where in your home you're going to keep your notebook, and make sure everyone knows where it should be found (if you have cleaning help, make sure they know where this belongs!). Ultimately, you'll want mini-versions of this notebook for each vehicle as well. If your home is multi-storied, you may want one on each level. If you have a basement, particularly one you might use during an emergency, be sure to keep a copy there as well.

Your Preaction™ Plan—Put It In Writing

Your plan is a working, living document; it's a tool to be implemented and revised as needed. Now, this isn't an English or creative writing class; no one is going to check for style, spelling or grammar. To facilitate this, we've included forms and a CD in this book; you can also download the forms at www.firestorm.com. A written plan accomplishes several things:

- *When you write something down, the very action of writing helps reinforce what you've written*

- *A written Preaction™ Plan makes it real*

- *A written Preaction™ Plan affords anyone access to it (make sure everyone knows where this is kept); better yet, make sure everyone who is a part of your Disaster Preaction™ Team has a copy*

- *Putting your Preaction™ Plan in writing means it will be easy to review and update as your situation changes.*

As best you can, you should fill out the forms as they appear in the book. Remember, the forms are meant as a guide, not the last word.

When you've completed a chapter, go to the forms in the book or at www.firestorm.com . There, you can either:

a) Fill them out on your computer and print the completed form; or

b) Print them off and fill them out by hand.

Ideally, you will populate your notebook as you go through each chapter. So, with every month, your notebook will continue to grow, until at the end of the year, it will become your reference in time of need. Other areas you may want to include, depending on your situation, might be:

- *Pets/livestock*

- *Additional input of any special medical needs*

- *Additional information about babies, seniors and people with mental or physical disabilities in your household*

Family Agreements

Along the way, you'll find we suggest several household agreements for everyone in the family to read and sign. Signing mutual accords/contracts lends importance to what you're doing in the minds and hearts of everyone involved. Why not create a ceremony out of these? Family ceremonies or rituals held around such agreements solidify your actions and do a lot to creating an inclusive, "we're-in-this-together" atmosphere.

FIRST FAMILY AGREEMENT—OUR CONTRACT

I, _____, understand that our family has acknowledged that some sort of disaster is likely to impact us. As a family, we have decided we want to be prepared for that eventuality.

I agree to take our efforts seriously, to encourage the rest of my family to do the same and to contribute to our plan in the best way I am able. This includes:

- *staying in open and honest communication about developing our Preaction™ Plan*

- *being present when our family meets to make or revise plans*

- *following through on any specific actions I take on*

Signature: _____

Date: _____

MONTH 1 ACTION PLAN

❑ Have The Conversation

❑ Complete "The Conversation" Form

❑ First family agreement signed by all

❑ Copy family routine and personal information onto index cards

❑ Prepare Preaction™ Plan binder(s)

❑ Congratulate yourself for getting started!

MONTH 1—CHECKLIST FOR THE CONVERSATION

How would you feel if a disaster hit our home today?

How would you know if a disaster crisis was coming or occurred?

What would you do if disaster struck right now?

Who would you call?

Where would you go?

How would you get there?

What would you take?

Begin To Assess The Actual Risks You Face

Start Working On Getting Prepared

❑ Inventory of flash lights, battery operated radio and batteries

❑ Inventory of food

❑ Turning off water main

❑ Turning off electricity

❑ Turning off gas

❑ Decide who will get the notebook and start setting it up.

❑ Agree to and set a date for a second meeting in two weeks.

★

2. IDENTIFY YOUR RISKS

There is an inverse relationship between
reliance on the state and self-reliance.
—William F. Buckley, Jr.

Most of us have never lived through a disaster. Many of us don't even know anyone well who has been through a disaster. But the numbers make it clear; each and every one of us is vulnerable to disaster.

FEMA (Federal Emergency Management Agency) lists 17 kinds or types of hazards that can result in anyone experiencing a disaster:

1. Dam Safety

2. Earthquakes

3. Extreme Heat

4. Fires

5. Floods

6. Hazardous Materials

7. Hurricanes

8. Landslides

9. Multi-Hazard

10. Nuclear

11. Terrorism

12. Thunderstorms

13. Tornadoes

14. Tsunamis

15. Volcanoes

16. Wildfires

17. Winter Storms

To these, we should add global pandemics like the bird or avian flu, power grid failures, as well as personal disasters, like sudden illnesses, accidents, identity theft, etc. The list is daunting. Of course, not everyone is subject to every hazard on this list or beyond. But, all of us are subject to disasters involving fire, water, hazardous materials, terrorism, pandemics, and weather-related incidents.

Real Risks

The November 2005 issue of Wired Magazine created a list of what might be America's next biggest disasters and the respective number of people who could potentially be affected. It looks, in part, like this:

1. Levee Break Sacramento

- Situation: 15 to 20 feet below sea-level & on river bank

- Hard Impact: Jeopardizes the water supply

- Likelihood: High—66 % ... When???

- Human Impact: 22 million

- Business Impact: Public & private companies, government, revenue & repair, History: New Orleans $60+ billion

2. Power Grid Failure—Northeast

- Situation: Shortage of new power plants & a growing population

- Hard Impact: New England poised for summer blackouts

- Likelihood: medium to high

- Human Impact: 40+ million

- Business Impact: last time in 2003 $6+ billion

3. Tsunami—Eastern Seaboard

- Situation: 1949 Canary Islands eruption caused the western Atlantic shores to slip a few yards into the ocean

- Hard Impact: a half-trillion-ton ridge slides further into the Atlantic, setting off a massive East Coast tsunami

- Likelihood: low—might not happen for a few thousand years

- Human Impact: Eastern Seaboard

4. Earthquake—Missouri

- Situation: 1811 New Madrid quake was the most powerful ever recorded in the lower 48

- Hard Impact: church bells rang as far away as Boston; St. Louis and Memphis still lack adequate earthquake building codes

- Likelihood: high—90% chance of a magnitude 6 or 7 tremor in the next 50 years

- Human Impact: 3.7 million

5. Meltdown—Indian Point

- Situation: nuclear reactor 35 miles from Manhattan

- Hard Impact: once evacuation orders are issued, people lack access to cars

- Likelihood: medium—once every 600,000 operational years or tomorrow

- Human Impact: 21 million

6. Tornadoes—Dallas

- Situation: tornado clusters at rush hour

- Hard Impact: nearly $3 billion in property damage

- Likelihood: medium—city has so far dodged the bullet

- Human Impact: 87,000 people in their cars, with additional 5.7 million indirectly affected

7. Flooding—Upper Mississippi

- Situation: shores are the most unstable locations for permanent structures

- Hard Impact: spectacular flooding approximately once every 20 years

- Likelihood: high—imminent; the last great floods were in 1993

- Human Impact: 72 million—everyone in the immediate floodplain

8. Eruption—Yellowstone

- Situation: geysers and hot springs powered by one of the world's most active volcanic systems

- Hard Impact: previous eruptions buried most of North America—Arkansas to Oregon & Canada to Mexico

- Likelihood: low, but not zero

- Human Impact: tens to hundreds of millions

9. Landslide—Mount Rainier

- Situation: "greatest U.S. volcanic hazard"

- Hard Impact: a moving wall of cement headed toward Puget Sound

- Likelihood: medium (such slides occur once or twice a millennium; the last was 550 years ago)

- Human Impact: 2.4 million

10. Rupture—Alaska Oil Pipeline

- Situation: over 1/3 of the supports are out of alignment due to melting permafrost

- Hard Impact: a loss of 850,000 barrels of oil/day or 11% of the nation's capacity

- Likelihood: low

- Human Impact: potentially, the entire U.S.

To some degree, each disaster risk is location-specific. But, for a more a realistic assessment of the actual risks you and your loved ones face, we have established Four Levels of Risk, or Four Zones:

- *Level 1—The National Zone—This is the whole country. Admittedly, there are few disasters of this magnitude, but a global pandemic is one that falls into this scope.*

- *Level 2—Your Regional Zone(s)—your town, city, or county… anywhere within a roughly 20-mile (32.2 kilometer) radius of your home. If you have a long commute, figure a second regional zone for your place of employment.*

- *Level 3—Your Neighborhood Zone(s)—a 3-mile (4.8 kilometer) radius of your home, your workplace and any schools your children attend.*

- *Level 4—Your Address Zone(s)—your actual home, your workplace and any schools your children attend.*

Determining Zones 2–4 will require some effort on your part, but it is easier than you think.

NOTE: Much of the information below contains web addresses. However, if you don't have Internet access for personal use you may find free access at your local library. Also, your children may be allowed to use these links in their classroom. In any event, we have provided the same information using alternative media.

Level 1—The National Zone—FEMA Maps and Overviews

The quickest way to get an overview of major natural hazards is to look at the maps provided by FEMA (Federal Emergency Management Agency). We caution you that these maps are large-scale and regional in scope… meaning, they are not in great detail; they are meant to provide general risk-assessment information and guidance only. For example, just because your address is slightly outside of an area that is subject to wildfires doesn't mean you're safe from them. FEMA has also written a book called, Are You Ready? An In-Depth Guide to Citizen Preparedness (FEMA Publication IS-22). Available in both English and Spanish, you can get your copy one of two ways:

1. Call 1-800-480-2520 to order a free single copy. Be patient; it will take several weeks to arrive. Despite the wait, the booklet is likely your best format, as it will be more portable (and save a tree, too, perhaps) as the downloadable file is huge (see below).

2. The full document (all 204 pages) can be downloaded from: http://www.fema.gov/areyouready/ (The Spanish version from: http://www.fema.gov/spanish/areyouready/index_spa.shtm)

As this is a large file, be sure you've got enough time and space (up 21 megabits) available for it to fully download. Nevertheless, we know you are anxious to get prepared, so we recommend you download the first two parts of Are You Ready? The first section, http://www.fema.gov/pdf/areyouready/natural_hazards_1.pdf helps you to determine local risks in the context of the following natural hazards: floods, tornadoes, hurricanes, thunderstorms, lightening, extreme storms, and cold.

The second half of FEMA's natural hazards overview is available at http://www.fema.gov/pdf/areyouready/natural_hazards_2.pdf. This section considers extreme heat, earthquakes, volcanoes, landslides, debris flow, mud slides, tsunamis or tidal waves, fires and wildfires.

As fires can affect everyone, and not all are natural hazards, each section, with the exception of that on fires, has a map of the country that indicates, in a general way, the risks found in each area. Print out each map that applies to you; if you're using the book version, bookmark each map you need, or make a copy of each one. We strongly suggest that you look at every map, if only to get a rough idea of your exposure. You may think you're not susceptible to earthquakes or volcanoes, but with one look at the map, you could be in for some real surprises, particularly with respect to flooding.

Level 2—Your Regional Zone(s)

A good first step in determining risks within your region is to ask yourself,

"What does everybody know about this area?" Chances are, you already have some insight into highways, manufacturing plants, dams, rivers, etc. Ask those around you, especially if they have lived in the area for a while, what they know about regional risks. You may learn about a previously unknown hazard.

Get a decent map (not a tourist one) of your city or town... any chain convenience store will have them. With a pencil and a piece of string, use the map's scale to mark off a 20-mile radius. Holding one end of the string at your address, and the pencil at the appropriate distance, draw a circle around your address.

A good resource for printable maps is (http://maps.google.com). Download a free program of Google Earth at: http://earth.google.com/. Here you can see your address and neighborhood in much greater detail. Google Earth will help you understand the physical lay of the land: geography and topography.

Note on your map locations of major highways and railroads (sources of possible hazardous waste spills and explosions) military installations, major airports and skyscrapers (potential terrorist targets), river beds (possible floods) and any other feature that catches your eye as a potential source of problems. As a wrap-up, using your regional maps and new knowledge, make a list of all the risks that apply to you.

Level 3—Your Neighborhood Zone(s)

If your family's home, school and work locations are greater than a 3-mile radius, do the following for all locations that pertain to you. You will need one map per 3-mile radius.

Start with the general list of risks you made in Chapter 1. To discover specific risks in your neighborhood, walk it. Do this more than once, to get a better sense of it. For a different perspective, if you have access to a car, drive slowly around this zone. Take your maps along. Note the distance you are from major highways, railroad tracks, railroad stations, warehouses (which might contain all sorts of hazardous materials), power plants, or airports of any size, in this evaluation. Are they upwind? or down wind from you? Keep an eye on the wind over time, so you're aware of which way it typically shifts. Should chemical spills, explosions or biological threats occur in your proximity, you could be affected, as winds carry their toxic vapors.

Is there a lake nearby? Is it above or below you? What about a river, or even a dry streambed that might be subject to flooding in severe weather? What about major water and gas lines? How about large power lines? Are there service stations close enough to be a threat if a gasoline storage tank blows up?

How far are you from help? Where is the nearest fire or police station and hospital? Could a bridge collapse prevent you from getting out of harm's way and where you need to go?

Look around you. What's next door on all sides? Businesses? If so, find out what they do at that particular location. If there's a green belt, determine if it's also a watercourse that might flood in severe weather. Do you face a major street? If so, dangerous commercial traffic could frequently travel this route.

Locate the gas lines on or near your property. Do they go out to the street or under your house? What about the power lines? Speak with your neighbors to learn more, and/or share with them what you've discovered yourself about the risks within your immediate vicinity. Each of you may have something to add to the other's findings, and you will then be better prepared for it.

Nuclear Power Plants

Currently there are 65 nuclear power plants in 31 states. They are listed below. If you live anywhere near one of these plants, you need to get ready for the possibility of a nuclear accident of some sort. Although the safety record of these plants has been good, it hasn't been perfect. The accident at Three Mile Island in Pennsylvania, in 1979, is proof of that.

Nuclear Power Plants (add this to the appendix)

1. Alabama: Browns Ferry, Farley (Joseph M. Farley)

2. Arizona: Palo Verde

3. Arkansas: Arkansas Nuclear One

4. California: Diablo Canyon, San Onofre

5. Connecticut: Millstone

6. Florida: Crystal River, St Lucie Turkey Point

7. Georgia: Hatch (Edwin I. Hatch) Vogtle

8. Illinois: Braidwood, Byron Clinton, Dresden, LaSalle County, Quad Cities

9. Iowa: Duane Arnold

10. Kansas: Wolf Creek

11. Louisiana: River Bend, Waterford

12. Maryland: Calvert Cliff

13. Massachusetts: Pilgrim

14. Michigan: Donald C. Cook, Enrico Fermi (Fermi), Palisades

15. Minnesota: Monticello, Prairie Island

16. Mississippi: Grand Gulf

17. Missouri: Callaway

18. Nebraska: Cooper, Fort Calhoun

19. New Hampshire: Seabrook

20. New Jersey: Hope Creek, Oyster Creek, Salem Creek

21. New York: Fitzpatrick (James A. Fitzpatrick), Indian Point, Nile Mile Point R.E. Ginna (Ginna, or Robert E. Ginna)

22. North Carolina: Brunswick, McGuire, Shearon-Harris(Harris)

23. Ohio: Davis-Besse, Perry

24. Pennsylvania: Beaver Valley, Limerick, Peach Bottom Susquehanna, Three Mile Island

25. South Carolina: Catawba, H.B. Robinson, Oconee, Virgil C. Summer (Summer)

26. Tennessee: Sequoyah, Watts Bar

27. Texas: Comanche Peak, South Texas

28. Vermont: Vermont Yankee

29. Virginia: North Anna, Surry

30. Washington: Columbia Generating Station

31. Wisconsin: Kewaunee, Point Beach

Make a more concise, but thorough list of all the risks you find in each zone or level. (In fact, you may even want to share this with your neighbor.) Now, with your list of risks, and using the resources suggested earlier, add detail about the actions you can take during each type of disaster. Each risk should be paired with specific actions per disaster. Review this with your family. Put your list in your Personal Disaster Preaction™ Plan notebook.

MONTH 2 ACTION PLAN

❏ Complete Risks in Each Zone

❏ Put a hard copy of this list in your Personal Disaster Preaction™ Notebook.

Don't get depressed or feel stuck here. The whole point of making the list is to put you in control. You can't prepare well for an emergency if you don't know your risks. This is a good step toward full preparation. What has this accomplished? You've prepared yourself to get prepared. Congratulate yourself on a job well done!

MONTH 2—RISKS YOU FACE FORM

Hazard or Risk	Distance from Neighborhood	Direction from House: N, E, S, W	Specific action to be taken in event of a disaster.
Level 1—The National Zone			
Level 2— Your Regional Zone(s)			
Level 3—Your Neighborhood Zone(s)			
Level 4—Your Address Zone			

★

3. YOUR CONTACT LIST

If you have to do it, you might as well do it right.
If it's worth doing at all, it's worth doing it right.
—Proverb

You want a solid hard copy of your contact list in your Personal Disaster Preaction™ Notebook so when an emergency does strike, you know exactly where the phone numbers you need are. Your contact list consists of three general categories:

1. Your extended family and any other personal support people

2. Emergency services like the police department, fire station, etc.

3. Business Contacts

Contacts: Extended Family and Friends

You already started your contact list when you made the list of your immediate family or household members, complete with information about where they are in a typical week. To that contact list add any family members in your region that are not yet on the list. Two or three families, particularly if you're in the same neighborhood, could collaborate to great effect in a real catastrophe. Contact information for reliable aunts, uncles, cousins and other friends who live within 100 miles are good choices.

Next, add relatives, friends and people you can count on (counselor, babysitter or spiritual advisor) who live more than 100 miles away. Include any who live outside the United States. These are your family and friends indeed! Ones you can really count on... no matter the distance. You want a solid list of quality people.

You need these people on your contact list for three reasons:

- *First, if a disaster hits you, they will be concerned and you'll want to notify them that you're okay.*

- *Secondly, if a major disaster hits and you're forced to evacuate, these people may be able to provide at least temporary housing and other resources for you.*

- *Finally, and maybe most importantly, family out of your area can act as communication points if you and your immediate family get separated and the local and cell phones don't work.*

If you haven't already done so, check with everyone on this list to make sure each understands what it means to be on your list, and that no one minds being on your list. Offer to reciprocate as well. This will help to spread the word that everyone needs to be prepared.

Contacts: Emergency Services

Your public and private emergency and non-emergency services providers include the following:

- Fire

- Police

- Sheriff

- Water

- Gas

- Power

- Ambulance

- Hospital

- County Health

- Phone—Landline

- Phone—Cell

- Doctor(s)

- Veterinarian

Jot down the emergency number, the business number, and the physical address for each agency and any individuals. (Note: some situations may be best handled through the business office instead of the emergency line). And, you've heard it before… based on your own assessment of individual risks you face, you may have to add others, so use the above suggestions as a guide only.

Contacts: Business

You should create a business contacts list as well. If you are a business owner, or have an active partnership or stake in one, include your key operational and other function-critical people, your accountant and lawyer. As an employee, ask your employer what the location-specific disaster plan is at your physical work address and how you will be notified in case of an emergency. If your place of employment has a crisis communications plan, get a copy and read it. Even if the company does not occasionally conduct unannounced drills, you'll know how you fit in.

MONTH 3 ACTION PLAN

❑ Complete your contact lists.

❑ Complete Emergency Services Form

❑ Put a hard copy of these lists in your Personal Disaster Preaction™ Notebook.

❑ Congratulate yourself for a job well done!

MONTH 3—EXTENDED FAMILY AND FRIENDS (WITHIN 100 MILES) CONTACT FORM

Name _____

Date of Birth _____

Landline _____

Cell _____

Business Phone_____

Email _____

Medical Info _____

MONTH 3—EXTENDED FAMILY AND FRIENDS (BEYOND 100 MILES) CONTACT FORM

Name _____

Date of Birth _____

Address _____

Landline _____

Cell _____

Business Phone_____

Email _____

Medical Info _____

MONTH 3—EMERGENCY SERVICES CONTACT FORM

Agency/Department _____

Address _____

Business Phone _____

Emergency Phone _____

Email _____

MONTH 3—BUSINESS CONTACTS FORM

Name _____

Date of Birth _____

Address _____

Business Phone _____

Cell _____

Landline _____

Email _____

★

4. YOUR FAMILY COMMUNICATION PLAN

The best place to find a helping hand is at the end of your own arm.
—Unknown Source

While there may be warning of some disasters, like hurricanes, most emergencies are unexpected. You and your family may be separated when disaster strikes. Children may be in school, adults at work. Even on weekends, active families tend to head in different directions.

You need ways to make sure you can find each other in the event of a catastrophe of one sort or another.

In Chapter 1, you made a list of the daily routines of your family members—who goes where, when, and at what time.

In Chapter 2 you listed extended family members and close friends who live in your community but don't live with you. Remember, ask permission of others to be part of your plan and apprise them of your intent as part of your plan. It is powerful and enabling to know you can count on people and equally so to be able to extend this generosity to others.

Who? The Lead

Decide who in your household will be the "lead" in a disaster. This person should have the ability to remain level-headed and calm during danger. Agree in advance who can guide quickly and rationally, and without conflict. This is your Lead. S/he is likely, but not always, the adult that has the most predictable schedule and the least out-of-town travel. By calling out a lead, you establish a chain of command. Have a backup Lead(s), in case the primary one is not available. Should something happen to your Lead, or s/he is not available, the second in command can provide the necessary direction and support.

Where? The Meeting Places

Identify where you and your family will meet when disaster strikes. Review how your family operates and the patterns you've discovered as you choose your meeting places. Meeting places do several things. They provide you temporary shelter at an agreed-upon location and give you a way to re-establish communication with your family. Most of all, they get you back in contact with those you need to be in touch with in an efficient, resourceful way.

Or, decide if you would rather not gather everyone together and instead prefer to keep everyone informed of each other's plans? Although everyone's first instinct is to head for home, this may not be the best choice, or even an option. Have alternate rendezvous points for work and home, if, for example, one commutes an hour away each day.

Once you've picked your primary location, choose a room within that location. If you've chosen your home, pick an interior room, or the basement—some place that is strong and provides minimum exposure. If you've picked a place other than your home, make sure you know the structure well, and don't forget to figure out how you will get in if it's locked.

Your Home

Your primary meeting place may very well be your home, but this may not be an available option. Some homes are more vulnerable than others… mobile homes are high-risk during tornados, low-lying homes are subject to floods and heavy storms, and wildfires present problems to homes in remote and not easily accessible areas. If you live in a high-rise, choose someplace close but at ground level. Be conservative when selecting your locations.

Getting Home When At Work

Consider how easy or difficult it will be to get to your primary meeting place from work. Does it really make sense to try and get there right away? Would it be better to stay at work or to find a safe place near work to hunker down until it's safe to move to your primary meeting place? If this is the case, make sure everyone in your family knows that is your plan.

Getting Home When At School

Coordinate your evacuation plans with the schools. Be sure your children understand both the school's plan and your own.

Make sure you understand what the school will do to protect your children while they are on campus. Whatever the state of preparedness (or lack thereof) at your children's schools, work that information into your own plans. For example:

- *Will the children be kept in their classrooms, or will they be gathered in some central location in the school campus? If so, find out where.*

- *Will the school attempt to get the children home or will they keep them on campus? At what point is that decision taken and how is this communicated to parents or guardians?*

- *If they're kept at the school, should you pick them up immediately or leave them there until there is less chaos?*

- *If you're picking them up, exactly where do you go? How will you find each other?*

- *If the school is forced to evacuate, to what location will they evacuate?*

- *What form of identification will be required to let you pick up your children?*

- *What happens if you can't pick up your children?*

- *How do you make arrangements for someone else to pick them up?*

If you've got teenagers who drive themselves to school, help them plan what they will do in various emergencies. Regardless of age, make sure each child knows the above as well, and periodically review this with him or her.

Alternate Meeting Places

Plan B is to have an alternate meeting place. If disaster forces you out of your primary meeting place, where will you go? This could be at the nearest street corner, or a specific address nearby that everyone can get to on foot.

Get a Plan B

- *Within the Vicinity*

If your primary meeting place is destroyed, or access to it is cut off, plan to meet up at another pre-arranged location. Often community centers or schools themselves are designated evacuation centers. Your local Red Cross can direct you to those in your area. To determine the best secondary meeting place for you and your family, consider patterns of movement, routines, schedules, times of year, etc. for each family member. Take into account what options each person has if…

- *S/he has no personal means of transportation?*

- *How will s/he get there if public transportation stops running?*

- *If the secondary meeting place is inaccessible, what is a third location at which to regroup?*

- *Out-of-Town*

This designated location, one that is out-of-town, could come in handy. This is the place everyone will head toward if your community is evacuated. One hundred or more miles away is a good rule-of-thumb. This is also the phone number(s) other family members will call if they get separated. Keep in mind that this location could be different for different disasters. For example, inland is safer from coastal terrain when faced with hurricane conditions, where anywhere along a threatened coast and its course headings would not be a haven.

When choosing your out of town meeting place, you also need to seriously consider the routes. If your community has an evacuation plan, get to know it. If everyone in your area is, for instance, headed north on the same freeway, you're facing gridlock and it may make better sense to stay home. We'll talk more about how to decide if it's better to stay or go in a later chapter.

Alternatively, check your contact list and see where you could go, if you're forced to evacuate your community. Talk over your choice with the person with whom you will be taking refuge to be sure s/he is in agreement with your wishes.

MONTH 4—MEETING PLACE FORM

First location:

Physical address _____

_____

Specific location at address _____

Landline _____

Cell phone _____

Email _____

Route Notes _____

Second location (Back-up):

Physical address _____

_____

Landline _____

Cell phone _____

Email _____

Route Notes _____

Third location (Another Back-up):

Physical address _____

_____

Landline _____

Cell phone _____

Email _____

Route Notes _____

Using your contact list, make a phone tree diagram of who is to call who during a disaster. The goal is two-fold:

1. To make sure everyone is notified during a disaster.

2. To reduce the number of calls during a catastrophe.

Each person on the list calls the next person and conveys the message. If that person is not home, leave a message and call the next person on the list. The last person on the phone tree should call the first person to ensure that the tree is completed and that the message was accurate. Your phone tree will probably look something like this:

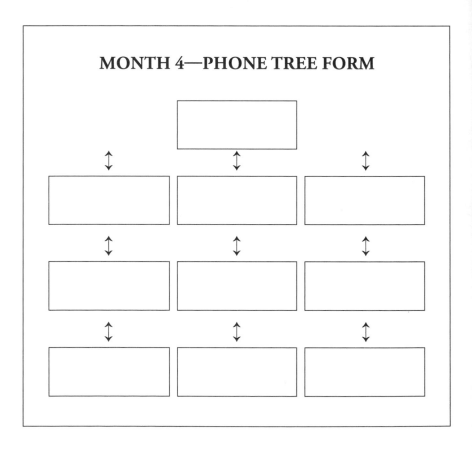

MONTH 4—PHONE TREE FORM

FIRST FAMILY AGREEMENT— OUR PHONE TREE

I, _____, understand that our family has created a telephone tree to be used in case of a disaster. A copy of this phone tree is attached to this agreement.

I agree to take our phone tree seriously and to encourage the rest of our family to do the same. I acknowledge that I know who I am to call should our phone tree be activated and agree to keep their numbers with me at all times. I also agree to update my phone numbers when necessary so our phone tree stays current.

Signature: _____

Date: _____

MONTH 4 ACTION PLAN

❑ Choose the Lead

❑ Complete your meeting places form

❑ Develop your family phone tree

❑ Sign Second Family Agreement – Phone Tree Agreement

❑ Put a hard copy of your meeting places form, phone tree diagram, and phone tree agreement in your Personal Disaster Preaction™ Notebook.

❑ Honestly evaluate your ability to evacuate

★

5. SHOULD YOU STAY...

The best lightning rod for your own protection is your own spine.
—Ralph Waldo Emerson

As you move forward with your preparations, bear in mind your particular circumstances. Having the right materials on hand in a disaster is critical to survival. And, with proper planning, you can even be comfortable. Your contingency preparations should be for at least three or four days, and longer if your situation allows. Let's start with the essence of life...

Water

Drinking/potable water is a requirement to sustain life. Under normal living conditions, we get a lot of water from our food, but when storing water, aim for half a gallon of drinking water per day per person. And, that's just drinking water. In an emergency, you'll also want water for cooking, bathing, and washing dishes and clothes. This adds another half-gallon/day, for a total of one gallon per person per day. Again, this is a minimum/day amount to have on hand. You may need to store more water if your specific risks warrant it. It's hard to store too much.

Storing water is pretty simple. You can store it in any clean plastic, fiberglass or enamel-lined metal containers. You don't need special containers—soda pop bottles, work fine. (Plastic milk jugs are hard to clean, so its best to avoid them.) If you buy bottled water, you've got the perfect containers. Fill them from the tap instead of throwing them out or recycling them.

Never store water in a container that's had toxic materials—you can't be sure you get it all. Glass containers are fine but they are vulnerable to breakage, and they are heavier than plastic to move.

Decide now where you're going to store water. A cool, dark place is ideal, but it should also be a place that's unlikely to be damaged and that you're able to get to easily. Think not only about how you'll move it to storage now, but how you'll get it if you need it. Water is heavy. A gallon of water weighs over 8 pounds.

Ideally, water should be rotated or refilled every six months. Figure out an easy way to put a date on each container the day you fill it. A marking pen can work; so can tape with the date.

Alternate Safe Water Sources

There's more water around your home and in many other buildings than you might expect. Consider your hot water heater and pipes as supplements to your stored water.

Water Heater

Water heaters usually have a spout for a hose attachment at its base to drain the tank. Your hot water heater may hold up to 40 or 50 gallons of water, so you'll either want to have sufficient containers available to hold that quantity or draw off a smaller amount a little at a time. If the latter is your case, it will help to have a second person at the nearest hot water valve inside to cut it off when your container(s) are full

To drain your water heater:

1. Turn off the gas or electricity.

2 Shut off the water to the water heater.

Caution! Wait for the water to cool!*

3. Attach a hose to the hose bib at the bottom of the tank

4. Put the other end of the hose in your container.

5. Open the pressure relief valve at the top of the tank by lifting the lever (leave it up, too).

6. If the water doesn't begin to flow, turn on a hot water faucet inside—that will start the hot water draining into your container.

7. Turn off the hot water faucet to stop the flow.

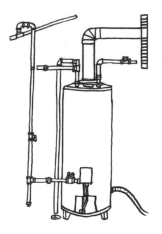

*This water may be very hot! It takes quite a while for the water to cool down once the heat source is turned off.

Know that water heaters contain sediment, undissolved minerals, and sand or other grit that originates from your water source. These deposits collect at the bottom of the tank, and sometimes this sediment build-up will block the drain hole. If this is the case, be sure the water is cool, then, with a screwdriver, coax the clog loose. Once the water starts flowing, set aside the first few gallons for washing and bathing, as these are likely to contain sediments, minerals, etc. as per above. When things return to normal, before turning on this heat source, remember to let your water heater fill up.

Pipes

There's always water in your water pipes. How much depends on the size of your home.

Here's how to get at it:

1. Turn off the water supply to your home (this prevents contaminated water from coming in).

2. Turn on the water faucet located in the highest point/floor in your home. A small amount of water will probably trickle out.

3. Take your containers to the lowest faucet—which may be outside—fill containers from there.

Exceptions: If you live in a single-story home, getting water out of your pipes can be problematic. Sometimes a garage is a bit lower than the rest of the house, which means any water faucet is likely to be lower too. Most single-family residences have a faucet outside, close to the ground, that's designed to drain the pipes. If you discover your water faucets are all at the same height, store more water.

If you're in a condominium or apartment, you may not have a shut-off valve to your unit or you may not be able to otherwise access this water source. Look for it; if you don't find it, contact the management office to determine where it is and if it's available to you in an emergency. If it's not, you need to store more water.

Water Sources to Avoid

NEVER drink:

- *Water that is discolored, has debris or unidentifiable substances floating in it, or has a foul odor.*

- *Floodwater. By definition, it travels over all sorts of places that are apt to be contaminated, picking up who knows what bacteria along the way.*

- *Salt water. The salt in sea water dehydrates the body, and it will kill you if you drink enough of it, however, salt water can be distilled for drinking.*

Treating Water for Safety

Rainwater, melted snow, running streams, natural springs and ponds or lakes can be safe sources of water, but you must first treat them. There are numerous ways to make water safe for your consumption.

Boil. If you have no other choice than to use water you haven't stored or drained from your pipes or water heater, you'll need to boil it for five minutes.

Bleach. You can also treat water with unscented, liquid household bleach that contains 5.25% sodium hypo chlorite. Note: bleach powder or color safe beaches won't work. Use 16 drops of bleach per gallon of water. Shake or stir the water, and let it sit for 30 minutes. If after that, the water doesn't smell slightly of bleach, treat again. If you're then still not getting a slight bleach smell, use that water only for cleaning, and then only if you must. (Some contaminate must have gotten into the water that the bleach can't handle.) Don't treat more than twice—using too much bleach can be poisonous and cause injury.

Boiling or treating with bleach will kill most microbes, but these procedures won't remove heavy metals, salt and other chemicals. That takes distillation. If your budget allows, purchase a water filter or water purifier—yes, there's a difference. Only purifiers render viruses inactive, using either an additional chemical or electrostatic process. Several sources for lightweight filtering and purifying equipment (this can be added to your escape kit) are outdoor gear stores, camping, backpacking equipment or other outfitter (hunter, fisher) stores. An online search will even give you more options. These same sources sell various chemical treatments like chlorine dioxide and iodine tablets, which also clean up questionable water. Note: filters are refillable and replaceable once they are spent.

Distillation

Distilling water removes all the microbes, salt, chemicals and heavy metals. Water is boiled, and the vapor of the boiled water condenses back into water. That condensed water is distilled and thus pure.

You can distill small amounts of water by filling a pot about halfway full. Tie a cup or other small container to the lid (usually the lid handle works) in such a way that the container hangs right side up, and not in the water, when the lid is put on the pot upside down. The shape of the lid will direct condensed water into the cup or container. Allow about 20 minutes to get the cup reasonably full. This is a labor-intensive method of getting pure water, and it requires lots of energy. But it is an option.

Compact solar stills cost around $200. You will find these at stores that cater to long-distance sailing crews or in an (this is obvious if minimally competent with the net) online search.

Food

When food supplies are limited, an average adult can get by for a long period of time on about half of what s/he normally eats. Infants and young children cannot, and the elderly or sick have their own special dietary needs.

In going about creating your stash, choose food that doesn't need to be cooked or refrigerated. This means canned, dried, freeze-dried foods and MRE's. MRE's (Meals Ready-to-Eat) were once only available to the military as daily rations, but the public can now obtain similar products. They are complete, balanced meals or meal components packed in nitrogen or oxygen. Some even come with heater packs. While expensive, they are portable, superbly packaged and practically last forever!

You may also find something similarly long-lasting and pre-packaged in your grocery store. Check the "prepared foods" aisle. Read the labels though, since some are more for long-term storage than others. This type of food is less economical than MRE's and more expensive than canned goods. Having said all this, you don't have to buy specially prepared food—you'll be unfamiliar with it, and it often doesn't taste very good. Instead, store three or four days of non-perishable goods in a cool, dark place.

Above all, select food that you like to eat and that falls in line with what you normally eat. Your food inventory should tell you how much of each type of food you tend to have on hand. Build from there, with these suggestions:

- *Canned fruits, vegetables and meats—those with pull-top covers eliminate the need for a can opener.*

- *Dried fruits and nuts*

- *Protein bars*

- *Healthy cereal (those with nuts mean added protein)*

- *Comfort food—trail mix, or easily portable foods that have good nutritional content for their caloric value, as well as a few "junk food" treats to boost morale.*

Food in the Freezer

As mentioned in Chapter 1, if you're home or someplace where there is food in a freezer, figure it will last up to 72 hours without power. There's variation in this number; it depends on how well the freezer is sealed, and the outside temperature, as well as how often you open it. You may be able to eat some of the food in the freezer without cooking it.

Cooking Outdoors

In a real emergency, you can usually expect to be without power. Yet, that doesn't mean cooking is off-limits. Having some way to boil water, make coffee and have a hot meal can do wonders for morale. If you get set up for cooking during a catastrophe, you can considerably expand your emergency food list. Barbecues are naturally at home in the outdoors. Backpacking and car camping stoves, fueled by small cans of propane, are inexpensive ways to cook outdoors, too.

Sterno® is a petroleum product often seen in special canisters keeping food warm at buffets. These small, lightweight containers provide cooking heat (only to about 200° F) for about 45 minutes, but that's enough to get a slow simmer going. Sterno also makes a stove that holds the can, making it a lot easier to use. This retails for around $10. You can find Sterno at supermarkets and both the stove and Sterno at hardware or sports stores. The Sterno stoves should be used outdoors.

Emergency Radio(s)

A battery-powered radio is the most reliable way to find out what's happening in a disaster. Extra batteries are a must. A self-powered radio that you run by turning a crank is another solution. Some even come with lights and a cell phone charger. A self-powered radio with the NOAA (National Oceanographic and Atmospheric Administration) weather channel, in addition to other features, is excellent. Emergency alert weather radios provide you with immediate information about life-threatening weather-related events. You can find these type of emergency radios at most local hardware stores, ranging in price from around $20-over $100, depending on features offered. Be aware that self-powered electronics may interfere with pacemakers.

Danger Notice for Manually Operated Self-Powered Devices

Former Surgeon General C. Everett Koop identified a potential concern with self-powered devices requiring a hand crank to produce energy to operate. The process of turning the hand cranks may produce electro-magnet fields that have the potential to disrupt a pacemaker. Please be aware of this risk. If possible, have some without a pacemaker operate the device. Do not hold the device in front of your body and/or immediately next to your chest will turning the hand crank.

Flashlights and Candles

You also need a few flashlights, candles, matches and lighters. Most flashlights need batteries, but some are self-powered using a crank, shake or lever of some sort to generate enough power to emit light. These are a wise investment at around $20. Look for a couple of sturdy flashlights that cast a decent light. You should consider one of each.

You'll need holders to safely use your candles. Keep candles away from drapes and other flammable items, and make sure they can't tip over. Tea lights are o.k. but don't last long. "Emergency" candles are more expensive than they need to be. You can easily find white, unscented utility candles that do the job, or pick some up at discount stores like Marshalls, T.J. Maxx, etc. The average burning time is often marked on the candle's packaging.

First Aid Kit

Every home should have a first aid kit. Although there are many so-called first aid kits on the market, many of them are not comprehensive enough to be useful. The American Red Cross suggests these items (For how many people? For what emergency?). Remember, this list is a guide. Depending on your particular needs, adjust accordingly.

- *(20) adhesive bandages, various sizes*
- *5" x 9" sterile dressing*
- *(1) conforming roller gauze bandage*
- *(2) triangular bandages*
- *(2) 3 x 3 sterile gauze pads*
- *(2) 4 x 4 sterile gauze pads*
- *(1) roll 3" cohesive bandage*
- *(2) germicidal hand wipes or waterless alcohol-based hand sanitizer*
- *(6) antiseptic wipes*
- *(2) pair large medical grade non-latex gloves*
- *Adhesive tape, 2" width*

- *Anti-bacterial ointment*

- *Cold pack*

- *Scissors (small, personal)*

- *Pocket knife (why quote the ARC when this is just common sense; yeah the quantities may be a bit off, but then again, we don't know how many this kit is for)*

- *Tweezers*

- *CPR breathing barrier, such as a face shield*

You can find a CPR breathing barrier online at reasonable prices. It will require some training. If you don't know CPR, get trained for free through many American Red Cross chapters. Your local fire department may also offer CPR training. This is a valuable life skill.

The rest of the kit can be purchased at a supermarket or drug store. Or, you can make one up yourself. You will spend about the same amount of money either way. If you create your own kit, you will usually end up with more supplies than the amounts listed above, but it will have taken your time, so it is a trade-off.

Add to this kit a selection of non-prescription medicines, like:

- *Aspirin or non-aspirin pain reliever*

- *Anti-diarrhea medication*

- *Antacid*

- *Syrup of Ipecac (use to induce vomiting in the event of poisoning)*

- *Laxative*

If anyone in your family is taking prescription medications, you'll want extra supplies of these, too, if you can get them. Talk with your doctor and insurance provider to see what can be done. If you have pets you don't want to discover you're out of pet food the day disaster strikes. The same is true of diapers or formula. Be sure you've got enough toilet paper, bleach, soap, menstrual pads or tampons, etc.

Store your first aid kit contents in such a way that their effectiveness is not compromised (excess heat or sun can damage and weaken their integrity), they are easy to get to in an emergency, and they are portable. A metal box, such as that for ammunition, is ideal, since it protects against moisture. This can be found in surplus stores.

Keep this first aid kit separate from the BAND-AID®-brand/other adhesive bandages and items you usually keep in your medicine cabinet or in the kitchen. Your disaster first aid kit is one you use only in a real catastrophe, not one that will get raided in the normal course of day-to-day living.

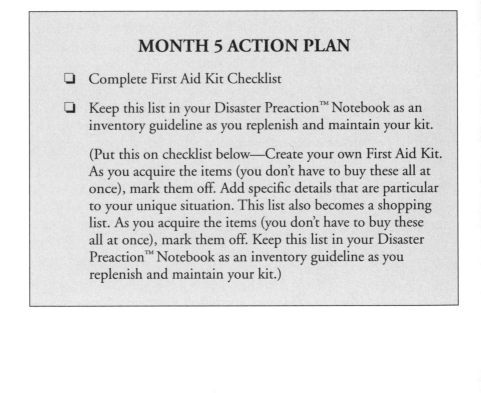

MONTH 5 ACTION PLAN

❑ Complete First Aid Kit Checklist

❑ Keep this list in your Disaster Preaction™ Notebook as an inventory guideline as you replenish and maintain your kit.

(Put this on checklist below—Create your own First Aid Kit. As you acquire the items (you don't have to buy these all at once), mark them off. Add specific details that are particular to your unique situation. This list also becomes a shopping list. As you acquire the items (you don't have to buy these all at once), mark them off. Keep this list in your Disaster Preaction™ Notebook as an inventory guideline as you replenish and maintain your kit.)

MONTH 5—FIRST AID KIT FORM

Item	Date Purchased	Date Stored	Expiration Date
☐ (20) adhesive bandages, various sizes.			
☐ 5" x 9" sterile dressing.			
☐ (1) conforming roller gauze bandage.			
☐ (2) triangular bandages.			
☐ (2) 3 x 3 sterile gauze pads.			
☐ (2) 4 x 4 sterile gauze pads.			
☐ (1) roll 3" cohesive bandage.			
☐ (2) germicidal hand wipes or waterless alcohol-based hand sanitizer.			
☐ (6) antiseptic wipes.			
☐ (2) pair large medical grade non-latex gloves.			
☐ Adhesive tape, 2" width.			
☐ Anti-bacterial ointment.			
☐ Cold pack.			
☐ Scissors (small, personal).			
☐ Pocket knife			
☐ Tweezers.			
☐ CPR breathing barrier, such as a face shield.			
☐ Aspirin or non-aspirin pain reliever			
☐ Anti-diarrhea medication			
☐ Antacid			
☐ Syrup of Ipecac (use to induce vomiting in the event of poisoning)			
☐ Laxative			

★

6. SHOULD YOU GO...

Look well into thyself; there is a source of strength which
will always spring up if thou wilt always look there.
—M. Antonious

Evacuation simply means leaving where you are. In a disaster there are two basic types of evacuation:

1. You need to evacuate or leave your home or workplace, but you can stay in the immediate area or community.

2. You need to evacuate your home, workplace, etc. and you must leave your community.

Either evacuation situation can happen with substantial warning, as in an oncoming storm or hurricane, or the need to evacuate can happen with no significant warning at all, like an earthquake, explosion or tornado.

Be Prepared!

The best way to prepare for any evacuation scenario is to assume you'll have little to no warning. With that in mind, build, in advance, an evacuation kit that you just grab on your way out. Work on this now, as you will NOT have time to do so when the warning comes, if you get any warning at all.

Your Evacuation Kit

An evacuation kit consists of the minimum basic survival materials you'll need in the two scenarios above. The components of your kit should be stored in a sturdy, but lightweight, portable container... one that is easy to carry and optimally water resistant. A backpack is ideal, because it leaves your hands free; one with wheels gives you the flexibility to wear it or roll it along, as required. A "wheelie" (carry-on suitcase with wheels) will also work.

You need not buy new backpacks and suitcases, i.e. check thrift stores or garage sales, or use an older one you already have. Before you choose your container, however, first determine and assemble the supplies you will include. That way, you will know what size container will be most appropriate for you.

Outfitting/Putting Together your Evacuation Kit

What supplies (gear and rations) do you need to include in your kit? Pack as if you had to carry the bag on your own on foot. Do not assume you will have access to a car. Given these guidelines, your evacuation kit should, at the very least, include:

- *Half a gallon of drinking water per person, per day*

- *Water for cooking, keeping reasonably clean, and for washing dishes and some clothes, about a gallon per person, per day*

- *Personal medical items: prescription medications, dentures and denture supplies, contact lens solution, etc.*

- *Emergency items: flashlights, batteries, candles, waterproof matches, emergency radio, first aid kit, and as much bottled water as it's practical to carry (2 liters is a reasonable amount)*

- *Cell phone and batteries*

- *Whistles: one light, cheap pocket whistle/per person that fits on a cord to wear around your neck. The sound of a whistle carries farther than your voice; establish a particular call, so you can quickly get your family's attention in a crowd*

- *Clothing: one change of clothes (including undergarments, socks and a warm jacket) per person*

- *Bedding: a sleeping bag or blanket or two or lightweight thermal blanket per household member and an inflatable pillow, if you wish. (thermal blankets are available from $4–10 each and are compact and reusable)*

- *Non-perishable, portable foods: protein snacks or trail mix*

- *A Swiss Army or Leatherman knife or hand-held multi-tool*

- *Cash: several hundred dollars, if you can spare it, as you may not have access to an ATM, or there could have been a run on the ATM, and despite you having money in the bank, the ATM may be wiped clean so that there is none to dispense to you*

- *An extra set of car and house keys that stays in your escape kit so you always know where one set is*

If you have infants or pets:

- *Baby items: several days' worth of diapers, formula, extra clothes and blankets*

- *Pet items: A carrier or leash and pet food for several days*

Important Papers

You need to be able to identify yourself (and sometimes your physical assets, like property and vehicles) to relief agencies.

- *Driver's license or other state-government-issued personal identification*

- *Passport*

- *Social Security card*

- *Proof-of-residence (deed or lease)*

- *Insurance policy and policy numbers and insurance provider emergency and non-emergency contact information*

- *Credit, charge and/or debit cards*

- *Bank account numbers*

A second set of important documents to have on hand (copies, that is) follows. These papers are a real headache to replace if lost, damaged or stolen.

- *Birth and marriage certificates*

- *Complete insurance policies*

- *Stocks, bonds, and other negotiable certificates*

- *Wills, deeds, and copies of recent tax returns*

Make copies of everything for your Personal Preaction™ Disaster Notebook. As paper gets heavy, two-sided copies will economize weight. If you find yourself seeking refuge in a public place, take great care to guard/ keep an eye on these items. An interior pocket of your backpack keeps such documentation from becoming tempting. Just like any personal property, your personal identity is subject to theft. Ideally, you should store copies of these documents away from your home, too, say in a safe deposit box. Knowing no place is 100% secure, mail another set of copies to a trusted out-of-town relative or friend. Upon filing your annual taxes, mail a copy to that designated person. Extend the same gesture to him or her who is doing you the favor.

Pack and Test

With all your materials together, pack them in your bag and walk around the block. If you can carry your kit with ease, it's about the right weight. On the other hand, if you find yourself struggling, take out some items (extra food, flashlight or cell phone), or divide the contents into two or more packs, so everyone but the smallest child carries something. In fact, your dog could even carry his/her own pack. If you build multiple evacuation kits, establish one pack as the primary kit. Put the non-essential items and extra food and water in the additional packs.

Extra Evacuation Kits... at Work

Put together an identical evacuation kit for your place of employment. Duplicate that kit for everyone who works outside the home. At work, the trick is finding a place to store it. If your employer provides you with a locker, great! If you've got a desk drawer that locks, place it there, or tuck it under the desk. To keep it from being stolen or accidentally taken for trash, make a smaller pack and put your name on it.

If there's no safe place to keep your kit, ask your employer. If you drive often for work, keep your evacuation kit in the car. If you're transported to various work locations, figure out the bare minimum you can keep with you at all times.

Extra Evacuation Kits... for your Car

If you have use of a car, this means you will have two to three equally prepared evacuation kits... one for your car, as well as the one(s) stored at home and/or work. The kit you leave in your car could include heavier items, such as canned goods (remember that manual can opener!) and extra water.

In addition to the more typical emergency items, a car also allows you to take with you useful tools. When buildings collapse, trees block roads and debris of all sorts collects in the most inconvenient of places/gets in your way, your tools could make a difference, or even rescue others. Of course, whatever tools you include, make sure you know how to operate them and are comfortable with your ability to do so. Consider these:

- *Hammer*

- *Folding lightweight shovel—(available at surplus stores and backpacking outfitters.*

- *Tire iron—there's usually one with your spare tire.*

- *Rope—a package or two of heavy duty clothes line will do the trick.*

- *A chain puller, ratchet puller, power puller—a hand-held "come-along" device that gives you a mechanical advantage when pulling, lifting, dragging etc. Small ones are priced around $12.00.*

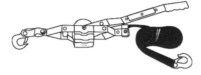

- *A light-duty portable saw (already mentioned) is expensive, but worth considering.*

MONTH 6 ACTION PLAN

❑ Prepare your evacuation kit(s), being sure to identify one as the primary to-go bag.

❑ Put your evacuation kit checklist in your Personal Disaster Preaction™ Notebook

❑ Batteries

❑ Bedding

❑ Clothing

❑ First aid kit

❑ Flashlight(s)

❑ Food

❑ Identification

❑ Keys

❑ Prescriptions, as necessary

❑ Radio

❑ Water

★

7. YOUR EVACUATION PLAN

*Your chances of success in any undertaking can
always be measured by your belief in yourself.*
—Robert Collier

If you had to evacuate, do you know how you would leave and where you
would go?

Almost every evacuation plan assumes one will have a car or other vehicle
in which to flee danger. The truth is, many people do not.

In cities, many rely on public transportation under normal circumstances,
but once something puts a kink in the system, there's no telling what kind
of service will be available to you. Despite an occasional nod to the use
of public transportation in some city evacuation plans, assess your own
situation based on how realistic you think those plans may be. In many
disasters, public transportation stops running completely.

For the most part, our country is not prepared to evacuate those who
have no access to their own vehicles. Given that, and the fact that, even if
you own a car, there's no guarantee you'll be able to use it (damage, lack of
fuel, inaccessible roads), work with your friends and neighbors to create
your own exodus plan.

Many preparations that will be useful during an evacuation have
already been done in Chapter 4, about two months ago, in your Family
Communications Plan. Now, the next step is to understand individual
evacuation scenarios.

To Stay or Go

The need to evacuate depends on many factors: proximity to the incident,
severity of such, prevailing winds (in the case of a chemical spill), landslide
or mud slide threats, flooding, etc. Some disasters, like hurricanes, flooding
or wildfires, are relatively slow to build, giving you time to evaluate your
options. Others, like tornados, terrorist attacks, or hazardous material spills,

develop quickly or without any warning or predictability.

Sometimes you'll get notice to evacuate from government authorities; often you'll have to make the decision on your own.

Evacuation Scenarios

Imminent Threat (No Warning/ Sudden Warning)—Leaving Home or Work

Example: A sudden event, like a fire or explosion that forces you out of the building, but you stay in the immediate neighborhood.

If something forces you out of your home or office but doesn't affect your neighborhood, your initial evacuation will likely be to the street. In Chapter 4 Communications Plan, review where everyone is to meet. When you can't return home, your most immediate challenge will be to find temporary shelter. Look to friends and families for lodging assistance or seek help from the local chapter of the American Red Cross. Remain calm, activate your Communications Plan, gather everyone together, and let the lead lead (or entrust decisions to your lead).

Short- to Mid-Term Threat (Limited Warning)—Staying in the Community

Example: A tornado where you may have limited warning, which may be only minutes, and you stay in your community.

From Chapter 4, you've already determined your secondary meeting place. Next, make sure everyone is clear on how s/he is going to get there. If you have a car, drive to your meeting place a few times. Since you may not have use of your car during an emergency, you should walk to your secondary meeting place at least once. Your perspectives and observations are different from a car than from on foot. Notice landmarks and how they could guide you if the streetlights are out. And, while landmarks are easy reference points, make note of their relationship to other things, for they may be down or otherwise unrecognizable.

Short-Term Threat (Some Warning)—Leaving the Community

Example: A major hurricane where you have some advanced warning and you leave your community.

As a general rule, the earlier you evacuate the better. If your community has established evacuation routes, get to know them, just as you did with the various routes to your meeting places. Using your best judgment, choose your evacuation route(s) and clearly mark each on a map with different-colored highlights. But don't limit your exit options to the planned routes. As these set or published ones could be grid locked, consider alternate routes, the so-called "blue highways." These are secondary roads marked in blue on the map to distinguish them from freeways and interstates. Using your best judgment, choose your evacuation route(s) and clearly mark each on a map with different-colored highlights. Keep one map in the car, away from sun and light, and one in your Personal Preaction™ Disaster Notebook..

Evacuation from Work

Probably the biggest issue in a disaster that requires you to evacuate at work is communicating with and getting back together with your family. Consider:

- *If only your work place is involved, how will you communicate to your family that you're okay?*

- *If the disaster is more wide-spread, how will you decide where to go—to your primary meeting place? Your secondary meeting place? Your out of town meeting place?*

- *Plan how to make use of your phone tree from work.*

- *Determine what you will do if phone communications are out.*

- *If you can't get to the chosen meeting place, what's your plan?*

Think it through! Talk over the details with your family and employer. If your workplace doesn't have any evacuation plans, make your own.

Disaster Planning at Work

Every employer should have a business continuity and disaster plan in place. Unfortunately, many employers are also in Disaster Denial. Start by asking what emergency plans your employer has.

If emergency plans are in place, get specific.

- *Ask what your employer expects you to do if your work location is damaged and closed.*

- *Ask what plans have been made if your workplace has to be evacuated.*

- *Ask how you're supposed to get in touch with your employer during an emergency.*

- *Ask how you find out if it is okay to come back to work.*

If you can get all your questions answered, all you have to do is match your employer's disaster plan with your Preaction™ Plan.

On the other hand, if you discover your employer hasn't made any plans or the plans are sketchy, offer to help. With the information in this book, you are equipped to help your employer start making plans to handle many disasters.

But you're equipped, right now, to get the process started. Your questions and your information may be just what your employer needs to get started on working on a disaster preparedness plan for your place of work.

Evacuation From School

If you have children in school, you need to know exactly what the school plans for disasters are. Be aware that many schools are still developing their evacuation plans and those plans are in a constant state of change. If you discover your child's school is lacking in emergency preparedness, help them get ready. You'll find school resources for this at the end of the book.

The problem from the school's point of view is what to do with the kids if they need to move the children from the school to someplace else. They need to be sure the children are picked up only by parents or other legally designated adults. They also need to have a place to take the children if they can't shelter them at the school.

You need to coordinate your evacuation plans with the schools. Consider:

- *If you're going to pick the children up, exactly who will do this?*

- *How will they get to the school or other location?*

- *What is your plan if you can't get to the school or other location?*

You also need to be sure your children understand both the school's plan and your plan. They need to be reassured that you've got the bases covered. It may make sense to choose a code word that only you and your children know; if someone other than you will pick up the children, give that person the code. Teach your children never to go with anyone who doesn't use the code.

Stay Informed

As you actively evacuate, draw on information you've researched and stay tuned to radio broadcasts. Updates will guide you to head north, south, east, or west.

The Emergency Alert System (EAS), formerly the Emergency Broadcast System (EBS), is a coordinated organization that provides emergency alerts across the country. You have probably seen these on TV: normal programming will be interrupted by a special tone followed by information scrolling along the bottom of your screen. Or, the radio will interrupt programming for a verbal alert. While a good procedure, it's unclear how effective this really is. Streaming online broadcasts are another source of real-time emergency notification and updates, if this communication is still available to you when you need it. Often, radio provides better local news coverage than television. You already have a sense of what your local media provides. Keep that in mind when choosing a source for news in an emergency.

MONTH 7 ACTION PLAN

❏ Fill out your evacuation plan forms

❏ Put them in your Personal Preaction™ Disaster Notebook.

MONTH 7—
PREACTION™ EVACUATION ROUTES FORM

… from home:

My final destination is:

_____

_____

_____

_____

_____

By car, my evacuation route is:

_____

_____

_____

_____

_____

On foot, my evacuation route is:

_____

_____

_____

_____

_____

MONTH 7—
PREACTION™ EVACUATION ROUTES FORM

... from work:

My final destination is:

_____

_____

_____

_____

_____

By car, my evacuation route is:

_____

_____

_____

_____

_____

On foot, my evacuation route is:

_____

_____

_____

_____

_____

MONTH 7—
PREACTION™ EVACUATION ROUTES FORM

... from school:

My final destination upon picking up so-and-so is:

_____

_____

_____

_____

_____

By car, my evacuation route is:

_____

_____

_____

_____

On foot, my evacuation route is:

_____

_____

_____

_____

_____

MONTH 7—
PREACTION™ EVACUATION ROUTES FORM

... from alternate school location:

My final destination upon picking up so-and-so is:

_____

_____

_____

_____

_____

By car, my evacuation route is:

_____

_____

_____

_____

_____

On foot, my evacuation route is:

_____

_____

_____

_____

_____

Repeat if you know where the children will be taken if they can't remain at school.

★

8. PROTECTING YOUR IDENTITY AND FINANCIAL INTERESTS

God helps them that help themselves.
—Proverb

Identity theft is a major concern. You should have a plan to protect your personal and financial information and monitor your credit status on a regular basis. We are concerned here with proving who you are and protecting your identity during a disaster or crisis.

Neither FEMA nor the Red Cross directly address the issue of identity theft, although both make it clear you need proof of identification to benefit from some of their disaster recovery programs. When you are displaced, you are out of your element and your normal guard is either down or to some extent compromised. Your faculties may not be that sharp, but remain alert. Be aware of your surroundings. You have on your person or in your kit important documents unique to you. Do not leave them unattended at any time.

Criminals and other mal-intentioned thieves thrive on (or take advantage of) this vulnerability. Identity theft can happen to anyone at any time. Not everyone who offers help is who s/he says s/he is. Nor do such unscrupulous individuals have your best interest in mind. In fact, ask whomever you are dealing with to identify themselves; write down their own personal and organization identity. Most people don't expect others to deceptively and illegally profit from them at their expense under duress, but it happens more often than not.

Sources of Identity Theft

Identity theft occurs when someone uses your personal information without your knowledge and/or against your permission. By representing themselves as someone other than who they really are, they commit fraud. Common sources that either alone, or in combination, can be used to deceptively trade off your goodwill are:

- *Credit, charge or debit cards or just the numbers themselves*

- *ATM, gas and department store cards*

- *Social security numbers*

- *Bank account information*

- *Telephone calling card numbers or cell phone account information*

- *Computer or online account logon and password information*

- *Utilities and other telecom/cable account information*

- *Driver's licenses, personal identification cards, passports*

Minimizing your Exposure to Identity Theft

Although there's a great deal you can do to protect your identity and financial information, you can become a victim through no fault of your own; however given the rampant criminal activity in this field, one cannot really prevent identity theft. However, you can reduce your exposure by keeping your personal information personal. How?

Watch Your Trash

Shred, burn or otherwise destroy any identifying information before you throw it out. Shredders are great, but you can also tear things up into small pieces. (With enough pieces of the puzzle, a good thief can recreate or complete your financial profile good enough to pass even the most rigorous of security checks and balances.) In short, beware what you throw away, no matter where you are. This includes:

- *Bills with account numbers*

- *Receipts of any kind with account numbers or partial account numbers*

- *Credit card solicitations or offers (even those fake solicitation cards)*

- *Credit cards (those of expired or cancelled accounts)*

- *Catalog labels (both inside and outside the catalog)*

- *Envelopes with your name and address on them (yes, even of all junk mail)*

Watch What You Say

When you're prompted to reveal identifying information, such as your Social Security number, your mother's maiden name or birth date, etc., before you respond, know with whom you are speaking. If you do not feel comfortable, keep asking until you get the information you need to divulge to them your personal information. Otherwise, hang up. In short, whoever solicits you should identify him-or-herself up front. If you must repeatedly ask for this type of information, s/he is not professional, and it would be risky to proceed. Instead, terminate the call. This is particularly the case if someone calls you. Your bank, insurance provider or credit card issuer won't call you for this information, as they already have it. If the call concerns a credit card or insurance offer etc., don't let them pressure you into giving them identifying information over the phone to take advantage of a "special deal" or "prize." If the "limited time" offer is legitimate, the company will mail you the application. It is not worth losing your hard-earned identity over a promotional gimmick.

Watch What Is On Your Person

Don't routinely carry multiple credit cards; take just the card(s) you need. The same is true of your Social Security card; you don't need it on a daily basis, so leave it at home. Besides, you've got the number memorized already, and the number is more often requested than the card itself.

Although keeping your driver's license and a credit card in your wallet is convenient, your wallet is the first thing an identity thief will attempt to steal. If you can, put those in a different pocket or a separate section of your purse. If your wallet is stolen, then all you've lost is your cash.

Watch/Monitor Your Accounts

Pay attention to your bank accounts, credit card statements and telecom and utility invoices. Often, you'll be the first one to spot a problem, based on your own known patterns of usage. Immediately report transactions you do not recognize. When you reconcile your checkbook, you'll be able to spot suspicious items on your statement. Spend a few moments reviewing all your credit card statements each month.

Take advantage of free credit reports. With each reporting bureau, you are allowed one free annual report (some states even allow two free per year, for a total of 6, or one every two months). Space those reports out so that every four months, you get a free one; this way, any inconsistencies are addressed right away. If an identity thief has set up a line of credit using a stolen identity, and has had the statements sent elsewhere, your credit report may be the first place to spot such suspicious activity.

As soon as possible after a disaster, check your credit report and all bank and charge, debit and credit card statements. If something appears out-of-line, follow up immediately. Also, if your credit card company calls you to verify recent charges that they think appear to be inconsistent with your spending patterns, DO call them back. That will ensure your continued, uninterrupted use of those funds. It is a minor inconvenience, compared to if they didn't inform you, and a thief went on a spending spree at your expense. It shows they are looking out for you, so work with them in detecting fraud.

There are other things you can do to safeguard your identity:

- *Get a locking mailbox, and keep it locked! Be careful who you give the key to, if someone checks your mail while you are on vacation.*

- *Request a mail hold with the USPS (they will do this for up to 30 days) With a mail hold, thieves watching your house will have a harder time determining if you are a soft target or not. Indoor light timers are a good deterrent. In summary, do not "advertise" that you are away.*

- *Place a temporary stop on your newspapers or have someone pick them up on a daily basis. The bottom line is to maintain the impression that your property is being monitored. Hence, do whatever you can to show activity at the site in question.*

- *Limit the information printed on your checks —avoid whatever identifying information you can. If you use a credit, charge or debit card, write "see identification" on the signature bar on the back of your cards (Note, some places, namely the USPS, will NOT accept cards that say "see identification;" if you want to pay with plastic there, your card must carry a real signature!)*

- *When ordering new checks, pick them up at the bank instead of having them mailed.*

- *When you travel, take extra precaution to protect your credit cards, passport, tickets, receipts, etc. Wear a money belt or similar item and make use of hotel safes. Many even accommodate laptops!*

- *Purchase a rider on your homeowner or renter's insurance policy that will provide both money and assistance, should you become a victim. Notify your credit and charge cards of where and when you will be traveling overseas. If you plan to purchase something that is outside of your normal spending history, let them know ahead of time so you are not embarrassed at the point of transaction. Note, however, that these days, you could be traveling and purchase something online, so the established patterns are getting harder to pinpoint, thus favoring identity thieves.*

- *When using public Internet café terminals log out of every site and close out of all browsers. Delete the search history. Do not leave a trace of your usage.*

If You Are Victimized

Don't let identity theft happen to you. Unfortunately, that is easier said than done.

The accidental and increasingly intentional (hackers, inside jobs) loss of information from data collection centers makes you vulnerable, despite all the precautionary measures you yourself take. If, however, you do become a target of identity theft, or suspect that you are a victim…

1. Call your credit and charge card companies. Your credit and charge cards have a toll-free number on the back. Of course, if your card is stolen, you will call the number you recorded earlier, since it's unlikely that you have the toll-free number memorized. Your statements also have this number and an e-mail address.

2. Call your bank(s). Do the same thing with any debit or bank cards you may have.

3. Call the police. Your local police or sheriff's department won't be able to do much about your stolen identity, but do file a report. Having a report on file with the police is a requirement for insurance and other claims, and it can expedite the recovery of the lost, misused or stolen items.

4. Call all three credit bureaus. Speak with someone in the fraud division at all three reporting bureaus. First call, then follow up with a letter that outlines your situation and reiterates your conversation with the phone representative. Do not rely solely on your call for someone on the other end of the line to accurately report your case. Be assertive and proactive.

- *Equifax: (888) 766-0008; P.O. Box 740250, Atlanta, GA 30374-0241*

- *Experian (Formerly TRW): (888) 397-3742; P.O. Box 1017, Allen, TX 75013*

- *Trans Union: (800) 680-7289; P.O. Box 6790, Fullerton, CA 92634*

5. Notify your Banks and other Providers of Extended Credit. Like charge cards, ATM and debit cards have a toll-free number on the back, as well as on your monthly statement. Make sure you've recorded that number someplace and keep it in your possession. If your checks have been stolen, call the bank at once.

6. Contact the Federal Trade Commission (FTC). The Federal Trade Commission won't help you resolve your individual situation; however, they do maintain a database that sometimes leads to law enforcement involvement. Filing a complaint with them helps to a) stop identity theft and b) track statistics by recording the increasing widespread recurrence and the stories behind each offender.

Call: (877) 438-4338

Write: Consumer Response Center
FTC
600 Pennsylvania Avenue, N.W.
Washington, DC 20580

Web: https://rn.ftc.gov/pls/dod/widtpubl$.startup?Z_ORG_CODE=PU03

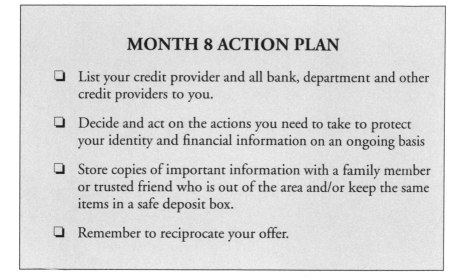

MONTH 8 ACTION PLAN

❏ List your credit provider and all bank, department and other credit providers to you.

❏ Decide and act on the actions you need to take to protect your identity and financial information on an ongoing basis

❏ Store copies of important information with a family member or trusted friend who is out of the area and/or keep the same items in a safe deposit box.

❏ Remember to reciprocate your offer.

★

9. MEDICAL FORMS

*The essence of intelligence is skill in extracting
meaning from everyday experience.
—Unknown*

Know your medical history, and enable others to know it, too, in time of need. If you're unconscious or otherwise unable to communicate, having the proper forms available can literally mean the difference between life or death. For each family member, prepare a concise documentation of the following:

- *Medical history*

- *Current medications and exact dosages*

- *Blood type*

- *Allergies*

- *Doctor(s)' contact information*

- *A recent photo (taken within the last six months) with the person's name, address and emergency contact number(s) on the back*

- *Identification: copies of your driver's license or passport.*

- *Medical release form*

If you need medical attention and have this information with you, the doctors can proceed; if not, you may be denied treatment. If your child needs medical attention, and you're not physically capable of providing this information, along with a medical release, such prepared documentation can act in your place. You do NOT want to waste time gathering this information when access to care is critical.

MONTH 9 ACTION PLAN

❏ Fill out in duplicate the following two forms and attach a photocopy or recent photo of yourself.

❏ Put each in your Personal Preaction™ Disaster Plan Notebook.

Personal Medical History
(Please complete a form for each member of your family.)

Name: _____

Birthdate: _____

Telephone numbers: _____

Physician: _____

Dentist: _____

Eye doctor: _____

Other: _____

Your current medical condition _____
_____
_____

List prescription and non-prescription medications you are taking: _____
_____
_____

Drug sensitivity and allergies (describe): _____
_____
_____

Name of health insurance carrier: _____
Group no.: _____
Agreement no.: _____

Have you ever been told you had one of the following?

	Yes	No
Lung disorder	☐ Yes	☐ No
High blood pressure	☐ Yes	☐ No
Heart trouble	☐ Yes	☐ No
Nervous disorder	☐ Yes	☐ No
Disease or disorder of the digestive tract	☐ Yes	☐ No
Any form of cancer	☐ Yes	☐ No
Disease of the kidney	☐ Yes	☐ No
Diabetes	☐ Yes	☐ No
Arthritis	☐ Yes	☐ No
Hepatitis	☐ Yes	☐ No
Malaria	☐ Yes	☐ No

Disease or disorder of the blood? (describe) _____
Any physical defect or deformity? (describe) _____
Any vision or hearing disorders? (describe) _____
Any life-threatening conditions? (describe) _____
Any contagious disorders? (describe) _____

(see next page)

Personal Medical History
(Page 2)

Have you been treated by a physician or been disabled or hospitalized during the last year? (describe)

_____
_____
_____
_____
_____
_____

Have you had or been advised to have a surgical operation within the last five years? (describe)

_____
_____
_____
_____
_____
_____

Date of last physical:_____

Date of last tetanus shot:_____

Family history—list important medical problems of your parents:

_____
_____
_____
_____
_____
_____

Mother:

_____
_____

Father:

_____
_____

Any other special medical information:

_____
_____
_____
_____
_____

★

10. WHEN YOU TRAVEL

In a crisis, be aware of the danger, but recognize the opportunity.
—John F. Kennedy

When you travel, you're often, if not usually, in unknown territory... out of the area for which you've done your disaster planning and preparations. Maybe even one where a foreign language or more are spoken. In most instances, you won't possess the local knowledge of area-specific risks, unless you've taken time to assess them before your departure. Except in the most general way, any evacuation plans you made at home don't apply when you're on the road. In these instances, there are, however, many things you can do to protect yourself and those traveling with you to be ready in the event of a disaster.

Leave your itinerary with two people

Identify someone who is not accompanying you and give him or her written details of your trip. This person becomes your Primary Travel Liaison. If you have any set appointments, give that person all the meeting arrangements and pertinent contact information. For each destination or leg of your trip, notify him or her of your safe arrival. Any time you change your stated plans while en route, and when you complete your trip, touch base with your liaison. Knowledge of your current whereabouts is mutually beneficial. When you check in with your liaison on a regular basis (establish what a "regular" basis is for you), you keep up-to-date about what's happening in both your hometown and your travel city. Assuming this person is on your disaster contact list, s/he will know how to get in touch with you should an emergency be happening back home.

If you are visiting friends and/or family or are on business, someone at your destination, your Secondary Travel Liaison, should have the same information as your Primary Travel Liaison. Critical information includes hotel, car, and tour reservations, as well as land, sea, or air transportation. Just as you keep the primary liaison informed of any changes to your itinerary and your safe return, you should maintain communication with your secondary one. Also, both Travel Liaisons should have each other's numbers. In short, whatever you do with Travel Liaison 1 as concerns your out-of-town whereabouts, do the same with Travel Liaison 2.

Note: this can be done without interrupting your vacation or otherwise getting in the way of you conducting business.

Before You Go—Think

When you're planning a trip, think about what you would do if disaster struck while you're traveling. This will increase your awareness so that if the worst happens you remain in a position to make good decisions. Before you leave, review the current social and political situations of your destination(s). The U.S. Department of State puts out travel advisories and warnings at http://travel.state.gov/, but you can do you own research by reviewing English-language publications online that cover local and regional news. If the worst happens, armed with your research, you'll remain calm and in a position to make rational decisions.

On a plane, review the emergency pamphlet in the seat pocket in front of you. Regardless of the number of times you have flown, when was the last time you paid attention to how many rows away you were (front and back) from an exit? On a boat, note the exits, windows, etc. Position yourself accordingly if you feel that the vessel is overcrowded and the passengers exceed the allowed capacity. This happens more frequently than you think.

Spend a few moments reviewing your Preaction™ Plan with the adults in your household. A calm assessment and a few reminders in advance will go a long way toward helping should a real emergency arise.

Document and Distribute

Prior to your departure, make sufficient copies of travel-related documentation. First and foremost, make four copies of your identification (one for family or friends, one for each liaison, and one to take with you). Keep your own copies separate from your wallet and passport. Depending on how well you know your liaison, provide him/her with the following:

1. Family contact phone list

2. Medical history & current prescription information

3. Driver's license number (write this down for yourself or have it memorized)

4. Serial numbers from your travelers' checks. You should also keep these numbers with you, separate from your wallet and passport.

5. Transportation tickets; plane, boat, train, bus (this should really be already found in a copy of your itinerary, which is mentioned above.)

6. Security and alarm codes and emergency/non-emergency contact information for both home and vehicle systems.

7. Your passport identification page (obvious)

Take only the credit, charge, debit and membership cards you actually plan to use. If you're traveling to South America, do you really need your Costco membership card?) Should something happen to your wallet, the fewer items you must replace means the less likelihood that an identity thief pieces together enough of your financial background to use it against you.

Have your mail put on hold. You can do this online at http://www.usps.com/ or use the yellow cards provided free by your post office. Also if you subscribe to a newspaper service, contact them to stop your newspaper delivery while you are gone.

Hotel Security

Upscale hotels with valet parking are generally the safest lodging options, but they are also the most expensive. The trade-off is that there is usually someone at that location with whom you will have come into documented contact (parking stub, check-in), and that person will have known your whereabouts at a specific time, should something go awry. Accommodations that are the most personal and individualized grant you this comfort. Nevertheless, even if cost is no object, there are times when you will be off the beaten path, which usually means less security. When deciding on your overnight arrangements, exercise caution at all times:

Parking

1. Park in well-lit lots close to the entrance of wherever you're headed.

2. Familiarize yourself with the route, noting freeway ramps and alternate routes, should you miss your intended exit/entry/turn.

3. If you don't have reservations and are driving, as you look for a hotel or motel, observe the neighborhood. Trust your instincts; if it doesn't feel right, drive on.

4. Hotel parking garages shouldn't have elevators that go directly to guest floors. The parking garage bank of elevators should only go to the lobby, with a separate bank of keycard-activated elevators giving access to the floors and rooms themselves.

5. Make note of where you park your car. Have your key out before you approach the vehicle.

6. If it's not a rental, do you have an extra set of keys?

Checking In

1. Key cards are safer than keys; if you're given a key with a room number on it, don't display it.

2. Rooms on the second to fifth floors are safer than those on the ground floor; rooms higher than the sixth or seventh floor generally can't be reached by emergency fire equipment.

3. Rooms that open to an interior hallway are safer than those that open to the parking lot.

4. Rooms with a window facing outside versus an interior atrium window can be reached by emergency fire equipment.

5. Rooms near elevators or stairways are safer than those at the end of the hall.

6. Know where the stairs are and how many doors are between your room and the stairs.

In Your Room

1. Look at the card on the door that shows emergency exits. Note your room's relation to the entire structure. Walk to all exits, pacing off the steps and forming a mental picture of distances

and other distinguishing features. If you don't understand the directions, call the front desk for clarification.

2. Locate the nearest fire extinguisher. (You should know how to use it from a similar one you have at home.) Count the steps to that, too.

3. Be sure you know how to use the phone.

4. Use the dead bolt at all times.

5. Do not post "Make up this room" signs. If you need your room to be made up at an unusual time, make arrangements with the front desk.

6. Use the hotel safe.

7. Use a door wedge, or jam a chair under the doorknob for extra safety. (If you've been given a key instead of a key card, the locks will probably not have been changed in a while.)

8. Identify anyone who knocks on your door before you open the door. If someone calls and says s/he is from the hotel and needs to enter to your room for any reason, get his/her name, and check it out with the front desk before you allow them in.

9. If a fire threat exists, check the door for heat prior to opening it; if the door feels warm or hot to the touch, leave it closed... chances are there is a fire on the other side. If there is heat or signs of a fire in the corridor, wet towels, bath robes and even sheets, and place them at the base of the door and around the jambs to keep out the smoke. For tight jambs, use tweezers, nail files, clippers or some other sharp object (yes, we know you don't fly with that pocket knife anymore) to secure a good hold. A knife from room service will do the trick.

10. Upon check-out, destroy your key card, as it contains personal information like your credit card and address. While encrypted to some extent, these cards are not "written over," until another guest uses it, so your key card exposes you to identity theft before it is re-populated with the next guests' information.

Packing

What you pack depends on the reason for and length of your stay and who is traveling with you; however, some basic guidelines are in order for most any journey.

1. The lighter you pack, the better. You are more of a target when you are loaded down with luggage than when you carry a single bag.

2. Dress and act conservatively. Avoid traveling with or wearing jewelry or displaying other signs of wealth (designer luggage, clothing, accessories, cameras, phones). Do not dress to draw attention. On the other hand, being too casual marks you as a tourist. While this is sometimes unavoidable, try to be nondescript and keep your voice low. Be careful with gestures, and never assume another person does not understand English.

3. Avoid handbags without secure closures, fanny packs and outside pockets on bags and luggage: Each is easy prey for thieves. A bag with a shoulder strap that can go across your chest is safer. Or, wear you backpack in front or to your side but pulled in front of you and secured with one arm. You may prefer a money belt or pouch that you wear inside your clothing.

4. Keep medicines in original containers: If authorities go through your luggage, which can happen at any international port of entry or exit (or even domestically), you want to be able to clearly demonstrate you're entitled to those medicines so that they are not mistaken for illegal drugs. If you're traveling abroad, take copies of your prescriptions, as well, making sure that they are legible.

Be Alert and Confident

Regardless of whether you are on familiar ground, awareness is your best defense.

- *Walk with purpose, and do not succumb to the unsuspecting ploys that abound in the more heavily- tourist areas. Each region has its specific con-artist tricks, and guide books often warn you of these. In hindsight, there are often obvious red-flags to their tactics. Be one step ahead of them, so you are not their next victim!*

- *When you enter a building, pay attention to exit signs and other departure points.*

- *If traveling in a group, have a meeting place and emergency plans for everyone.*

- *Note hospitals, urgent care facilities, police and sheriff stations, etc. Chances are, you'll spot these with little effort.*

- *If you see evacuation route signs, note the direction they are pointing and their nearest cross streets.*

- *Keep your cell phones charged. If you carry a wireless device, make note of coffee shops and other places where wi-fi connections are available.*

In summary, know what's around you, and assess your immediate environment. Once you get into a pattern of awareness, it will become second nature.

MONTH 10 ACTION PLAN

❏ Determine your Primary and Secondary Travel Liaisons. Speak with them about their roles, and offer the same gesture to them.

❏ Double-check your emergency kit; be sure to replenish it upon return of each trip, and modify its contents, depending on the type of trip you are taking, the time of year, and other relevant factors.

★

11. PANDEMICS

*Wisdom is knowing what to do next, skill is knowing
how to do it, and virtue is doing it.*
—David Starr Jordan

As this book goes to press, international and national news are full of worry about bird flu, also known as avian flu and the H5N1 virus. For our purposes, the name of the potential pandemic isn't nearly as important as the fact that a global pandemic of one sort or another is almost a certainty. Pandemics last months, even years. While a pandemic is a relatively slow moving disaster, once it latches on in your area, it moves quickly.

There are two schools of thought regarding the outcome of Y2K planning and preparedness. You either believe the whole issue was hype, and there was no reason for all the expenditure, since nothing happened or you believe that it was all the effort, expenditures and hype which caused nothing to happen. Regardless of where you fall, there is no question that a corporation would have been negligent not to have taken precautions. The same is true of the potential avian flu pandemic.

Whether you believe that the avian flu pandemic is not going to materialize as a worldwide threat, or that the devastation will be so widespread that planning is not possible or you are too busy to think about it, our family needs you to develop a plan. Currently The World Health Organization is on the verge of raising the Pandemic Alert from Phase 3 Level, "no or very limited human to human transmission", to a Phase 4 Level, "evidence of increased human to human transmission".

Every day the threat from the H5N1 virus increases. The number of fatalities from the virus has increased over threefold this year alone, and currently one person is dying every two days from the disease in Indonesia alone. Recent evidence of human infection has been found in China and Russia as well as many Third World countries. The virus will continue to mutate and infect people around the world.

Historically, there have been three pandemics every century for the last

1000 years. Statistically, the likelihood of a pandemic from this virus is 96%, within the third standard deviation.

Whether this is the virus which will create the next pandemic is irrelevant. There will be another one and it is incumbent on everyone to be prepared. Corporations' Officers and Directors will be judged using the "business judgment" rule. Ask at work or school what is their pandemic plan.

It is possible that you could choose to do nothing and assume the risk of a pandemic. This decision must be made after due consideration of the exposure so that appropriate diligence can be argued.

A Preaction™ Plan that includes an avian flu makes sense. The "prudent man" standard, applied to negligence actions, would suggest that if there are known, predictable risks, which are not addressed, you are not doing your job in protecting your family.

The pandemic of 1918, which this company survived, killed 675,000 people in the United States. The "W" shaped mortality curve shows that the working population is not safe. Everyone knows people who will lose loved ones. The 1918 pandemic killed 2% of the world population. Today that would exceed 120 million people. The current virus is more virulent and is killing more than half of the people who come into contact with it. The human impact as projected by The Center for Disease Control, The World Health Organization, and The Federal Government will represent an absenteeism rate of over 40% for over 3 weeks at a time in 3 separate waves. Your family's well being and earnings would be severely affected. There are ways, however, to limit this exposure.

Whether you believe it will occur or not, every individual has an obligation to at least be informed of this issue. The real question to be answered is whether to lead or follow? Whether the preparations themselves have value? Whether the amount of money spent will be recouped many times over, even if there is no pandemic?

Most of the planning which will be done to create an effective response to the avian flu is the same type of planning and preparation which will apply to many other man-made or natural disasters.

At the moment, influenza or "the flu" is considered the most likely to cause a pandemic. It is so potentially dangerous because the source virus mutates rapidly, making it almost impossible to prepare an effective vaccine in a timely manner. Couple that with the fact that a person infected with the flu can travel around the world before s/he even realizes s/he is sick, infecting many of those with whom s/he comes into contact on the way, the probability of a global scale crisis is obvious. If the avian flu evolves as expected, to human-to-human transmission, it's estimated that it will spread throughout the US in 10 days.

A pandemic creates more problems than more typical disasters, like hurricanes, wild fires, severe winter storms, tornados, and earthquakes. The July/August 2005 issue of Foreign Affairs magazine said this in the summary to an article titled "Preparing for the Next Pandemic" by Michael T. Osterholm:

> *"If an influenza pandemic struck today, borders would close, the global economy would shut down, international vaccine supplies and health-care systems would be overwhelmed, and panic would reign… "*

This sounds extreme until you realize that there is no adequate vaccine against the bird flu. If a viable vaccine were developed today, there would not be enough supply produced in time to avert disaster. As borders close and chaos takes over, supplies of food and other critical supplies will be interrupted, as state and local authorities try to stop the spread of illness. In other words, martial law is a possibility. Given this, determine how you would prepare for 3 months to a year of unrest/chaos. Buying in bulk would relieve some tension.

The United States has done some planning. On November 1, 2005, President Bush announced the National Strategy for Pandemic Influenza. The document says, in part:

The National Strategy for Pandemic Influenza guides our preparedness and response to an influenza pandemic, with the intent of (1) stopping, slowing or otherwise limiting the spread of a pandemic to the United States; (2) limiting the domestic spread of a pandemic, and mitigating disease, suffering and death; and (3) sustaining infrastructure and mitigating impact to the economy and the functioning of society.

It also spells out how this will be accomplished…

- *Where appropriate, use governmental authorities to limit non-essential movement of people, goods and services into and out of areas where an outbreak occurs.*

- *Provide guidance to all levels of government on the range of options for infection-control and containment, including those circumstances where social distancing measures, limitations on gatherings, or quarantine authority may be an appropriate public health intervention.*

What you can do

The first step in getting prepared for a pandemic is to establish habits of prevention. Regardless of a threat or not, the following are lifestyle changes that you should incorporate as part of your personal daily habits. Form good habits now, and teach everyone in your household to do the same. The more preventive action, the better we all are for it.

1. Cough or sneeze into a tissue. If you don't have one, do so into the bend of your elbow. This keeps germs off your hands. Or, bend deeply at the waist and cough toward the ground. Both prevent the spread of infectious droplets.

2. If you're sick, stay home.

3. Get a flu shot. Note, the typical flu shot will not protect against avian flu, but it will reduce your risk of more common strains of the common flu; which in turn reduces your vulnerability to other illnesses, including bird flu.

4. Exercise, eat healthily to boost and maintain your immune system, and do not smoke or drink excessively.

MONTH 11 ACTION PLAN

❏ With a pandemic in mind, review your Disaster Preaction™ Plan.

❏ Make any adjustments to it that you feel would be appropriate, in light of possible movement restrictions, incapacitated or overwhelmed emergency responders, etc.

★

12. KEEPING YOUR PLAN CURRENT

Self-reliance is the only road to true freedom,
and being one's own person is its ultimate reward.
—Patricia Sampson

First of all, congratulate yourself. You now have your very own Preaction™ Plan. As things in your personal life change, so, too, will your plan; however, it's not just the family dynamics that change… neighborhoods and whole regions do as well. A new freeway opens, a military base closes, evacuation routes are changed, a community center is built, and a chemical manufacturing plant opens nearby. Each of these events, and any like them, also requires an amendment in your Preaction™ Plan and notebook. The most efficient way to keep both your items current is to review and update them on a monthly basis. We suggest you pick a set day of the month, say on the 12th, so that it becomes a routine. It's the kind of habit that can pay big dividends.

Conversation and Practice

A monthly conversation over dinner with the whole household is the best way to make sure everyone remains on the same page regarding readiness. Give yourself about an hour to talk about any changes that have occurred. As a guide to your discussion, have everyone bring his/her notebook. This will move the conversation along more quickly, and with it on-hand, you're also not likely to overlook anything. Flip through each tab, calling out any points that require updates. Record any relevant changes in your Preaction™ Disaster notebook.

These review and practice sessions can be fun and reassuring. Look at them as becoming a productive family ritual. The key is to stay prepared.

Practicing Your Plan

Reviewing your plan involves periodically practicing a few elements of the plan itself. (maybe you should bullet these?) Some things, like your contact list, need reviewing every month. Others will require action only every three or six months. If you practice, when something does happen, you'll know what to do without having to give it much thought. Practicing also reveals any flaws in the plans. So, without delay, and using the lists below, schedule when you will perform each, and write that date down on your calendar.

Every Month

- *Discuss any family, neighborhood and/or regional changes you know have taken place, and update as needed.*

- *Review your contact list and phone tree.*

- *Check every evacuation kit(s), and make needed replacements and adjustments.*

- *Check your supply of batteries, candles, matches and/or lighters.*

- *Test your emergency radio and flashlights.*

- *Test smoke detectors.*

Every Three Months

- *Quiz everyone about:*

  —calling 911

  —turning off gas, water and electricity

  —location of emergency kits

- *Renew your inventories of food and water.*

- *Walk to your secondary emergency shelter. We mean everyone! Not only will this ensure you know the route, but in most areas of the country, you'll experience it in different weather.*

- *Hold a fire drill, and meet at the designated corner.*

Every Six Months

- *Review stored food.*

Annually

- *Replace smoke detector and smoke alarm batteries.*

- *Test and recharge your fire extinguisher(s) according to manufacturer's instructions.*

MONTH 12 ACTION PLAN

❑ Congratulate yourself for having diligently prepared your Personal Preaction™ Plan over this past year.

❑ Schedule all reviews for the coming year (monthly, quarterly, semi-annually, annually)

CLOSING—WHAT'S NEXT?...

★

AFTER A DISASTER

Our greatest glory is not in never falling, but rising every time we fall.
—Confucius

The wildfire is now put out, the storm has passed, the earth has stopped shaking, the chemical spill is contained, the volcano is no longer rumbling... Now, your job/focus/responsibility is on recovery. Just how you recover, and how long it will take, depends on the type of disaster you've experienced. Part of preparing for disaster is anticipating what you will do after it ends. Look at the recovery in post-disaster stages, so as to not get overwhelmed.

- *Immediate recovery*

- *Short-term recovery*

- *Long-term recovery*

Post-Disaster

Immediate Recovery

First and foremost, remain safe. Is the event completely over? For example, the earth no longer quakes, but damaged buildings may continue to fall; the hurricane no longer dumps rains, but the levees then fail.

- *In some cases, law enforcement officials and emergency personnel may be in a position to tell you it's safe to re-enter certain structures. In many cases, however, the aftermath of a disaster is as chaotic as the disaster itself, and they will not be available, at least initially. Don't panic; use common sense.*

- *Gather your family—this is your mutual support system; make plans together.*

- *Handle immediate medical needs—check everyone for wounds or injuries. Use your first aid kit and/or seek additional treatment.*

- *Avoid obvious hazards—downed electric lines, the smell of gas, standing water, etc. Make sure everyone remains alert and knows how to spot and stay away from danger.*

- *Listen to your emergency radio—use it to determine your next moves, which may be to remain where you are. Be careful of rumors; they can exacerbate a disaster, leading to unnecessary risk or pandemonium.*

- *Defer making major decisions—focus on the present; when your life is suddenly in upheaval and your status quo is interrupted, you will not be in the frame-of-mind to make sound decisions. But, don't worry, for the emphasis now should be on your immediate needs. You will not gain anything by deciding or feeling pressure to decide something under duress.*

- *Expect emotional reactions—emotions run high after a disaster and swing back and forth. Some people are elated, because it's over; others are depressed, because things are such a mess. Fear is likely to continue for some time. Do not ignore these feelings and reactions as they come up; address them with love and understanding.*

- *Take in enough food and water—provided you still have your reserves, stay hydrated and nourished in order to maintain energy and stay as comfortable as possible.*

- *Stay off the phone—lines will be jammed, if they are working at all. Conserve your cell phone batteries.*

Short-Term Recovery

Once you're sure the disaster is over, you move into the short-term recovery phase. Again, your first job is to stay safe. During this period (which could be anywhere from a few hours to several weeks), keep providing emotional support to each other, as the healing process is gradual.

Depending on the kind of disaster you've gone through, at this point, you'll need to start making some decisions. Do you or can you return home? Or do you need to find temporary housing? In doing so, do not rush to any conclusions. Calmly and rationally assess your situation. Now may be the time to activate your contact list.

It's during this time that outside help will probably begin to arrive. Local emergency services people will probably be first on the scene, followed by state representatives, and, if the disaster is large enough, eventually FEMA and other Federal resources. Remain alert, as there will still be a great deal of confusion. The various assistance agencies might not be communicating and coordinating well with each other, which means you may get conflicting instructions and information. If someone, even an official, tells you something that doesn't make sense, if at all possible, wait before you act on that information. Before long, the situation will begin to clarify itself.

Long-Term Recovery

For a particularly severe event, recovery can take time, and lots of it. In fact, it can take years before a community regains a sense of normalcy. Emotional reactions really set in at this stage. Children, even some adults, may suffer from nightmares or depression. The disaster preparations you made and practiced will help through this tough time. If the concerns persist, seek professional guidance; there is no shame in doing so.

Again, keep your cool, yet stand up for yourself when that's required. Be as flexible and resourceful as the situation warrants. Speed-up/Expedite the recovery process with your identity papers and financial records. If for some reason they are not in your evacuation kit, access those that you mailed to a friend and start things moving forward.

CONGRATULATIONS!

Congratulations! You should feel good about what you've accomplished. You and your family have gone from disaster denial to disaster preparedness. Now, share that knowledge gained. Help a friend or distant family member start his/her own Preaction™ Plan. Organize your neighbors to create a neighborhood Preaction™ Plan. To the extent that you can, lend support and insight to those around you who are just now embarking on preparations to become their own first responders.

DISASTER PREPAREDNESS—RESOURCES

There is an amazing amount of public information out there about preparing for a disaster, with the most current being online. There is also much duplication, so go to these resources first, as we have found them to be the most helpful.

American Red Cross—Disaster Preparedness

http://www.redcross.org/services/disaster/beprepared/—general information, as well as that specific to seniors. Washington headquarters: (202) 303-4498. Your local Red Cross is listed online or in the phone book.

American Red Cross—Disaster Preparedness for People With Disabilities

http://www.redcross.org/services/disaster/beprepared/prep.html— information specific to those with disabilities

Wikipedia

http://en.wikipedia.org/wiki/emergency_preparedness—largest reference web site on the internet—very informative

Medline Plus—Disaster Preparation and Recovery

http://www.nlm.nih.gov/medlineplus/disasterpreparationandrecovery.html— brings together authoritative information from the National Library of Medicine, the National Institutes of Health (NIH), and other government agencies and health-related organizations

DHS (U.S. Department of Homeland Security)

http://www.ready.gov—information categorized by businesses, families and children

FEMA (Federal Emergency Management Agency)

http://www.fema.gov/areyouready or *http://www.fema.gov/spanish/ areyouready/index_spa.shtm*—contains emergency response and planning information. Documents on various hazards can be downloaded along with fact and planning sheets.

http://www.fema.gov/pdf/areyouready/natural_hazards_1.pdf—helps you to determine local risks in the context of the following natural hazards: floods, tornadoes, hurricanes, thunderstorms, lightening, extreme storms, and cold

http://www.fema.gov/pdf/areyouready/natural_hazards_2.pdf—considers extreme heat, earthquakes, volcanoes, landslides, debris flow, mud slides, tsunamis or tidal waves, fires and wildfires

Google

http://maps.google.com—good resource for printable maps

Google Earth

http://earth.google.com/—downloadable free maps

DPERA (The Disaster Preparedness and Emergency Response Association)

http://www.disasters.org—multi-lingual site linking disaster professionals around the world

U.S. Department of Education

http://www.ed.gov/admins/lead/safety/emergencyplan/crisisplanning.pdf—a free downloadable book to help schools prepare for disasters

HHS (U.S. Department of Health and Human Services)

http://www.hhs.gov/emergency/index.shtml—disasters by type

Firestorm Solutions, LLC

http://www.firestorm.com/book/book.html—a .pdf version of this book

The Flu Wiki

http://fluwikie.com—information about all types of flu

Are You Ready? An In-Depth Guide to Citizen Preparedness (FEMA Publication IS-22).

INDEX

12 Step Overview 7
12th of each month 14

avian flu, bird flu 20, 32, 105–108
after a disaster 113–114

contact lists
  business 45
  emergency services 44
  family 43

declaring a disaster 19
disabilities 21, 23, 27, 117

epidemics 14
evacuation
  decision to 75
  from community 52, 69, 76–77
  from home 69, 76
  from schools 78
  kit at work 72
  kit for cars 72
  plan 10, 14, 50, 52, 75–84

families
  single-parent 22
  with infants and children 22
  with older children 22
  with seniors 23
  with disabled household members 23

FEMA (Federal Emergency
Management Agency) 17, 31, 35–36,
115, 117–118
fire 9, 12, 17–20, 22–23, 31, 36, 76,
101–102, 110–111, 118
first aid kit 64–67, 70, 113
food
  cooking 57, 62–63, 70
  in the freezer 25, 62
  inventory 24, 62

forms
  medical 93–96

identity
  theft 32, 85–91, 101
  personal papers 71, 115
inventory 24, 62

meeting places
  alternate 51
  out-of -town 52

pack and test 72
pandemic 14, 20, 23, 32, 35, 105–108
pets/livestock 21, 27, 65, 71
phone tree 54–55, 77, 110
plans
  Communication Plan 13, 49–55
  Evacuation Plan 10, 14, 50, 52,
  75–84
  Personal Disaster Preaction™ Plan 40
  Preaction™ Plan 28–29, 108, 111
practice 109–111, 115

recovery
  long-term 113, 115
  post-disaster 113
  short-term 113–114
resources 117–118
risk
  assessment 35, 45, 98
  levels 35–38

supplies
  flashlights and candles 11, 63
  food 10, 12–13, 24–25, 57, 61–63,
  65, 70–72, 107, 110, 114
  personal medical 70
  radio 13, 24, 30, 63, 70, 74, 79,
  110, 114
  tools 73

water 10–13, 17–19, 25, 32, 38, 44, 57–61, 63, 70, 72–73, 110, 114

travel 10, 89, 97–103

hotel security 99–101

liaison 97–98, 103

packing 102

updates
  monthly 13–14, 109–111
  quarterly 111
  semi-annual 111

utilities
  electricity 25, 30, 58, 110
  gas 25–26, 30, 38, 44, 58, 110, 114
  water main 18, 25, 30

water
  distillation 61
  requirements 57
  pipes 18, 25, 58–60
  purification, treatment 60–61
  sources 58–60
  storage 11, 12, 57

zones, identifying
  Exact Address 35
  National 35–36
  Neighborhood 35, 37–38
  Regional 35–37

FOOTNOTES

1. http://www.ciwmb.ca.gov/Disaster/DisasterPlan/chp14.htm#sectionone

2. http://www.redcross.org/services/prepare/0,1082,0_91_,00.html

3. http://www.foreignaffairs.org/20050701faessay84402/michael-t-osterholm/preparing-for-the-next-pandemic.html

4. http://www.whitehouse.gov/homeland/pandemic-influenza.html

NOTES

James W. Satterfield,
President/Chief Operating Officer, Co-Founder Firestorm Solutions, LLC

Mr. Satterfield has extensive experience in public and private companies in leading the identification of problems and designing solutions. He has been President, CEO, and COO of various public and private companies in dealing with insurance, reinsurance, technology, communications, and environmental issues. Under his leadership, he was instrumental in establishing underwriting guidelines, policy development, claims and pricing procedures and rating structures. Jim achieved significant growth and improved profitability in his M&A, sales and business development responsibilities.

He has lead in the development of national standards for pollution prevention, risk management, and environmental due diligence. He is currently directing disaster due diligence for public companies and helping them cope with disaster denial.

He has both an undergraduate engineering and Masters in Science Degree from The Georgia Institute of Technology.

Harry W. Rhulen Esq.
Chairman/CEO, Co-Founder Firestorm Solutions, LLC

Mr. Rhulen spent the first eighteen years of his career in the insurance industry. He has worked as a consultant in many industries, using his risk management, crisis management, and business management skills, public company, legal, bankruptcy, and due diligence experience to help his clients. He has been Chairman and CEO of a public insurance holding company with United States and European operations. Mr. Rhulen has extensive due diligence experience having participated in over thirty M&A transactions. He has lead several public offerings raising in excess of $350 million.

Mr. Rhulen, as an insurance industry representative, serving on the board of the American Insurance Association, testified before Congress to expand the opportunities for financial service companies. He has served on the boards of several profit and not-for-profit entities. He has received humanitarian awards for many of his efforts, including the "Quality of Human Life" Award from the American Red Cross. He graduated Cum Laude from the College of Insurance and has both a Juris Doctor and Masters of Business Degree from Syracuse University.